HEINRICH HEINE

POEMS OF
HEINRICH HEINE

(Revised Edition)

THREE HUNDRED AND TWENTY-FIVE POEMS
SELECTED AND TRANSLATED

BY

LOUIS UNTERMEYER

Author of *Challenge, Roast Leviathan,
Modern American Poetry*, etc.

NEW YORK
HARCOURT, BRACE AND COMPANY

COPYRIGHT, 1917, BY
HENRY HOLT AND COMPANY

COPYRIGHT, 1923, BY
HARCOURT, BRACE AND COMPANY, INC.

PRINTED IN THE U. S. A. BY
QUINN & BODEN COMPANY, INC.
RAHWAY, N. J.

THESE TRANSLATIONS
ARE GRATEFULLY DEDICATED
TO
HERMAN EPSTEIN
TEACHER AND FRIEND

PREFACE

In his " Life of Heinrich Heine " (one of the hasty but surprisingly excellent pot-boilers written before his *alter ego,* Fiona MacLeod, became a cult), William Sharp points out what he considers Heine's " fundamental and puzzling complexities."

Among other and less significant things, he recognizes him as a romanticist and the chief foe of Romanticism; a true poet and a born journalist; an historian without method, a philosopher without a real philosophy; a free liver and yet loyal to his wife and reverent of his mother; the most tender of Teutonic poets and the most brutally cynical; a German, yet the bitterest scourge of Germany; an intense admirer of Sterne, a lover of Shakespeare, a commender of the poets of England, and a hater of the nation and everything English; a cynic who laughed at sentiment, and a sentimentalist in spite of all things —impatient and irritable in health, of heroic endurance in ills more terrible than ever fell to the lot of a poet. . . .

Some time before this, even before the death of Heine, Gerard de Nerval had written: " It is no idle paradox to say that Heine is both hard and soft, cruel and tender, *naif* and sophisticated, skeptical and credulous, lyrical and prosaic, impassioned and reserved—an ancient and a modern." . . . But neither Nerval nor Sharp made anything but a perfunctory and half-perplexed attempt to explain this amazing discovery of contradictions. Sharp, in particular, wound up his book with a rapt appreciation, ending in a flourish of rhetorical trumpets, and concluded the matter.

But it needs something more than a list of antitheses to understand this restless genius, a confusing figure who has been paired with such names as Catullus, Aristophanes, Burns, Rabelais, Cervantes, Voltaire, Swift, Villon—in fact to every writer who is known as a master of either simplicity or irony. It needs a close and interpretive reading of his "Book of Songs"; it needs a general knowledge of the politically experimental and altogether chaotic times of which he was so fiery a product; and it needs, first and last, the constant reminder that Heine was a sensitive Jew, born in a savagely anti-semitic country that taught him, even as a child, that "Jew" and "pariah" were synonymous terms. The traditions and tyrannies that weighed down on all the German people of his day were slight compared to the oppressions imposed upon the Jews. The demands upon them, the petty persecutions, the rigorous orders and taboos would form an incredible list. Let these few facts suffice: In Frankfort, when Heine was a boy, no Jew might enter a park or pleasure resort; no Jew might leave his ghetto after four o'clock on a Sunday afternoon; and only twenty-four Jews were allowed to marry in one year. In such an atmosphere Heine received his heritage of hate and his baptism of fire.

A great deal of literary nonsense and general confusion has resulted because so many of Heine's critics and biographers have taken him at his own valuation. Heine was never, as he so often and fondly thought himself, a Greek. He was not that fictional creature, an Hellenic Jew. Nor was he, except in a geographical sense, a French or a German Jew. He was, in spite of the seemingly absurd redundancy, a Jewish Jew.

In a crude generality, one might say that the Greek ideal was decorative, the Jewish ideal was social. The Greeks were glad to create work that brought happiness to the creator; they produced, in the best sense, 'Art for Art's sake.' The Jews were never satisfied with so exclusive and aristocratic an aim; their motto (if they ever had one) might have been 'Art for Life's sake'; for, from the first prophet-priests who compiled the Books of Moses to the obscure rhapsodist who wrote the Psalms, the vision was always a democratic one. These Jews identified themselves with their songs; their confident egoism as message-bringers lifted them above their preoccupations as artists; and when they exalted God they were celebrating what was godlike and powerful in men. Before the Jews would acknowledge Beauty, it would have to stand shoulder to shoulder with them, work among them, drink, sweat, suffer and become part of their daily desires and dreams; to them it could never be merely its own excuse for being. The hotly humanist element in Heine stood out constantly against the deliberate, unimpassioned and cool reserve of the classicist.

The Jews, as he himself so frequently pointed out, are an inherently insurgent, stubborn and uncomfortable race; a people whose temperament is almost directly opposed to the overrefined consciousness and Olympian serenity of the Greeks. And Heine was even more 'insurgent, stubborn and uncomfortable' than the most typical of his race.

Heine imagined he was 'a joyous Hellene' because

he recaptured something of that strange mixture of æstheticism and Homeric splendor; because he sang, in a worldly and mechanistic age, of Aphrodite, nightingales and a defiant paganism; because he addressed his literary prayers to Apollo rather than to Jehovah or to 'the melancholy Nazarene.' These things, of course, made him no more truly Greek than the putting on of a toga would have made him a Roman. Compare, for instance, his familiar, rude and altogether human manner of treating the deities (in "The North Sea") with the way they are treated by a truly Hellenic poet like Landor. And every chapter in his score of prose volumes, every page of his careless and often bantering letters, every line of his direct and intimate poetry, shows him for what he was: the unusually emotional and quick-tempered Oriental: the true Semite, never so sensitive as when he covers his hurt with a cynical shrug or a coarse witticism; his rudest jests being often the twisted laugh of a man in agony.

The man Heine (if one can consider him for a moment without regard to his race or his gifts) recovered from his early love-affair with his fickle cousin in Hamburg. Heine, the Jew (aggravated possibly by Heine, the poet) never did. On the contrary, he dwelt on the theme and magnified it until it not only colored but dominated all his poetry. Not once, but a hundred times (and with surprisingly few variations) does he tell the story of the faithless and calculating girl who married not for love but for money. He becomes bitter with each thought of it; all the Jew in him leaps up in anger and ironic pathos whenever he thinks of what, to any one else, would have seemed no more than a youthful betrayal. In what is undoubtedly the keynote to this self-inflicted torture, he turns to answer the woman, and, incidentally, the world. *"Vergiftet sind meine Lieder?"* he expostulates:—

> "My songs, they say, are poisoned.
>   How else, love, could it be?
> Thou hast, with deadly magic,
>   Poured poison into me.
>
> "My songs, they say, are poisoned.
>   How else, then, could it be?
> I carry a thousand serpents
>   And, love, among them—thee!"

And he is characteristically the Jew, not alone in his overheated hatred but in his equally hot and luxuriant desires; his voluptuous love of the color and flavor of things, his feverish imagination (a source of sharpest pain as much as of intense delight), his confident egoism—all of which is as pronounced in the Jew to-day as it is loudly proclaimed in the Old Testament. At one time he writes, "The history of the Jews is tragical; and yet if one were to write about this tragedy he would be laughed at. This is the most tragic of all." And, at another time, he is gaily asserting the Jews' ancient and unconquerable superiority. He hails, with an almost personal pride, the superiority of a race that watches its proud contemporaries with the same ironic mixture of terror and toleration that it watched the once proud kingdoms of antiquity; knowing them all to be, like the vanished Egyptians, Persians, Romans, tyrannical—and transient. It is this hand-in-hand-with-God attitude that is behind Heine. It is the old confidence that makes him, even in this slight and little-known poem, express the spirit of a race:

> "What! Think you that my flashes show me
>   Only in lightnings to excel?
> Believe me, friends, you do not know me,
>   For I can thunder quite as well. . . .
>
> "Oaks shall be rent; the Word shall shatter—
>   Yea, on that fiery day, the Crown,
> Even the palace walls shall totter,
>   And domes and spires come crashing down!"

"Germany," his greatest prose work, and "Pictures of Travel," his most popular, are full of the same mingling of scholarly poise and boyish impudence; the same abrupt shifting from intense passion to careless, or careful, mockery that is never absent from his poems. Time and again he builds a structure of the deepest and most poignant emotions only to pull the foundation from under and let the whole thing come tumbling down with a flippant or ridiculous last line. Nor was this petulance a literary sham. Even on his deathbed, when an officious priest advised him to make his peace with God lest he die unforgiven, "I am not worried," Heine said, "*Dieu me pardonnera; c'est son metier.*"

It is the shrug that masks his agony, and one must understand this shrug not as an affectation but as a symbol. It is with a shock of delayed recognition that we realize the bitter sharpness of so many of the verses, whose keen edge familiarity has dulled. "You have diamonds and pearls; you have all that men desire. And you have also the fairest of blue eyes—my love,

Preface

what else can you wish for?" Thus, innocently begins the famous "*Du hast Diamanten und Perlen*"—and we scarcely think of the poem's fierce undercurrent because we are hearing it for the thousandth time set to the genial measures of a *gemüthliche* folk-tune.

And it is this very folk-song quality, the same spirit that ranks him with Burns, the unknown minstrels of Spain, and England's border balladists, that insures him his permanence as a poet. Things like "*Die Lorelei*," "*Du bist wie eine Blume*," "*Lehn' deine Wang' an meine Wang'*," and a hundred other brief but overwhelming lyrics are immortal for their very obviousness. They seem to have nothing to do with literature. One cannot trace their origin or find their beginnings in books. They seem an unconscious part of the world's speech; as if they always were—born when the language was, with none of the labor of the artist or the file-marks of the craftsman about them.

And this, possibly more than anything else, makes Heine's triumph the greater; for never were a poet's results more carefully planned. Far from being fortuitous, the slightest of his verses were subjected to the most minute and ceaseless changes. To attain that baffling and inevitable naturalness, he would rewrite a quatrain as many as six or seven times, simplifying it with each new version. No poet ever hated more than he the commonplaces and accepted conventionalities of poetic formulæ, the *clichés* and inversions, the archaisms and affectations that have no relation to anything but a stilted and æstheticized literature. He was in this like Herrick and Villon and Burns who, as Synge points out, used their daily speech and their own personal life as their material; and the verse written in this way was read "by strong men, and thieves, and deacons, not by little cliques only."

"Don't prettify me!" Whitman said to Traubel, when told of his intended biography. Heine had no Boswell to admonish; he was his own commentator. And he saw to it that the world should have no shiny, smooth and dressed-up portrait of him;—in fact, he uglified himself. To give a complete picture of himself as a man, he overemphasized his coarseness, dwelt too lovingly on his carnal vices; but, with all his most democratic intentions, he found it difficult to reconcile himself to the world and impossible to reconcile the world to him. His highest ambition was to help build a greater and consolidated Germany—and his works were interdicted in his own country! He counted his poetic gifts little beside his fervor for liberty. He wished to be remembered, not so much for his songs, which gave their deathless impetus to Franz, Jensen, Schubert, and particularly to Schumann (in whom they found not only their greatest composer but their most creative interpreter), but for his struggles toward democracy. These struggles and his hatred of complacent customs find expression in all his essays no less than his verses. He was as much disgusted with cant and stale formulæ when he found them in politics as when he met them in poetry. As in the prolog to "The Harz Journey," he voices his contempt for the "laundered bosoms" and "polished salôns," so in all his prose sketches, his reviews and even his letters, this contempt gathers and grows. He longed for the overthrow of smug respectability, for the end of autocracy in government no less than in art. "It must perish," he wrote, "it has been judged and condemned, the old social order—let it meet its due! Let it be destroyed, the old world where cynicism flourished and where man was exploited by man. Let them be utterly destroyed, these whited sepulchers, where lies and injustice have had their dwelling place." This fire of enthusiasm, sweeping through a wasted frame, almost burnt itself out. So fierce was its vigor that Heine often suffered the inevitable revulsion. Physically unfit to mingle with and enjoy crowds, Heine by turns distrusted, feared and scorned the mob. He looked on 'a communal future' with an apprehensive bewilderment and misunderstanding that even his satire could not disguise. A year before his death he wrote, "I can think only with anxiety and terror of the time when these dark iconoclasts will have gained power. With their horny hands they will heartlessly smash the marble statues of beauty so dear to my heart. They will destroy the fantastic toys and spangles of Art which the poet loved so much. They will cut down my grove of laurels and plant potatoes in their stead. They will tear from the soil of the social order the lilies that toil not nor spin. . . . The same fate will befall the roses, those idle brides of the nightingales; the nightingales, those useless singers, will be driven out—and alas, my 'Book of Songs' will be used by the grocer to make the little paper bags in which he will wrap coffee or snuff for the old women of the future." But though the possible triumph of the proletariat momentarily distressed him, Heine was always the impassioned radical. Proud of being a poet, he was prouder of being a protagonist. "Poetry," he wrote in a triumphant sort of climax, "has always been to me a consecrated instrument, a divine plaything, as it were. And if ye would honor me, lay a sword rather than a wreath upon my coffin—for I was ever a fearless soldier in the war for the liberation of humanity."

And this poet, who helped bring a nation toward freedom, was born chained to his race, and could never escape from himself! The paradox of his life is the thing that helps to clear all the foregoing carefully-assembled paradoxes. Matthew Arnold has expressed something of it in his "Heine's Grave":

> "The spirit of the world
>   Beholding the absurdity of men—
>   Their vaunts, their feats—let a sardonic smile
>   For one short moment wander o'er his lips.
>   *That smile was Heine!*"

And what made that smile even more tragic was the fact that Heine recognized it. Never for a moment could he forget how sardonic it was.

II

But one other fact must be borne in mind to understand Heine and his work—the fact of his sickness. The sharp turn of his utterance was not alone caused by a mental twinge, but by a physical twist. Occasionally, perhaps, the spirit of the outcast Jew ceased suffering. Not so his body. That was continually being racked and tortured. "Many a time," he wrote to his friend Varnhagen von Ense, "especially when the pains shift about agonizingly in my spinal column, I am moved to doubt whether man is really a two-legged god, as the late Professor Hegel assured me five and twenty years ago in Berlin. When the harvest moon was up last year, I had to take to my bed, and since then I have not risen from it . . . I am no longer a divine biped; I am no longer 'the great Heathen, number 2' . . . I am no longer a joyous though slightly corpulent Hellene, smiling gaily down on the melancholy Nazarene. I am now only an etching of sorrow, an unhappy man—a poor, sick Jew."

If Heine's 'spiteful and exaggerated bitterness' still rouses any one's resentment, it should be remembered that besides what his doctors diagnosed as "consumption of the spinal marrow" he was afflicted with debts and enemies. Before he was fifty, he was half blind, lame, without the sense of taste or smell; his lips were paralyzed, his ears were quick to catch any discordant sound (for years this sensitivity had to endure an amateur violinist's practicing) and he was desperately poor besides; misunderstood, maligned, defrauded and deceived.[1] This agony, which ended in an eight years' crucifixion on a mattress grave, was with him from the beginning. Even as a boy it afflicted him; it discolored his imagination and perverted his youthful fantasies. We see the results of it in the preternaturally gloomy "Dream Pictures" and in his "Youthful Sorrows" (significant titles both!) written between the ages of sixteen and twenty-one. It heightened and distorted that romanticism which Heine alternately worshiped and mocked. "The thousand years' reign of Romance is over;" he wrote to von Ense. "I myself am its last fairy-king." The classic period had come to an end with Schiller and Goethe, and the Romantic school was dying of its own extravagances and exaggerations. Kleist, Rückert, Uhland, Wilhelm Müller, Eichendorff and Chamisso, that remarkable Frenchman

[1] *Vide* William Sharp's "Heine," Chapter VI.

who wrote more genuinely German poetry than most of his Teutonic contemporaries,—all of these were loosely joined by the bonds of a tender and patriotic romanticism. With a wealth of color and splendid imagery, Heine surpassed the entire group; using their very mechanics, he wrought a strange, new music from the old material—and then proceeded to laugh at the artifice of the entire structure. He utilized, with a fresh power and a more imaginative realism, all of the old paraphernalia and properties before discarding them. Sphinxes, moonlight, ruined gardens, nightingales, enchanted roses, dead lovers arisen from the grave, wild horsemen, dancing skeletons, giants, mermaids, loreleys and suicides appear and reappear throughout the poems; but a keen sophistication appears with them. " Heine may be said to be the last of the celebrated German Romantic School, the funeral pyre of which he himself helped to build up in his youth, only to set it ablaze later on with the scorching flame of his own remorseless wit. And, behold, from its ashes arose a strange phœnix, the anti-romantic and modern spirit which justly entitles Heine to be called one of the deliverers of thought, the champion of progress, and the sworn foe of all stagnation." [1]

This creative irreverence, accompanied by a disillusioned fantasy and often wanton caprice, creeps into all his prose. Sometimes it even overpowers his larger, political writings. But more often it lifts and illuminates them. Heine's individual quality pervades and flavors his voluminous works, whether he is recording local French affairs, writing essays on ' Shakespeare's Maiden and Women,' jotting down journalistic

[1] From Kate Freiligrath Kroeker's' "Memoir" in her *"Poems selected from Heine."*

Preface

sketches of England, reviewing a musical season, criticizing the French Salôn, satirizing German literature and German thought, inditing venomous letters or penning a series of exquisite and immortal travel-pictures. The sardonic flashes, the exuberant fancy, the interplay of philosophy and wit makes all he wrote pungent. But it was the poet in him that makes it poignant.

III.

This poignancy is naturally at its deepest when Heine's rôle was his natural self; in his poems. And, at the risk of being redundant, I repeat that one must continually keep in mind Heine's life and his love-story to understand his poetry to the fullest. For (and here lies the greatest difficulty for the translator) his apparent simplicity often hides an inverted introspection. Most of the poems only half express his meaning; sometimes they do not actually express it at all. Morbidly sensitive and secretive in his life, Heine was equally so in his verse; time and again he makes his lines talk around his thought rather than on it. Even the simplest and most apparently obvious of the love-songs have a hidden suggestion far deeper than their *naïveté*. See, for a few varied examples in "*Die Heimkehr*" alone, Number 4 (*Im Walde wandl' ich und weine*), Number 28 (*Was will die einsame Thräne*) and the often translated classic Number 47 (*Du bist wie eine Blume*). This last, for instance, is not the bland, sentimental love-song that it is so often taken for. In the first place, it should be evident from the context, no less than its content, that it is not addressed to any sweetheart but to a very young girl, possibly a child. Seeing the innocent beauty of this flower-like creature (*so hold und schön und rein*) he longs to lay his hands on her forehead, and pray God to keep her always as at present, "so sweet, so fair and pure." One can almost hear Heine taking a breath in his last line; as if, with a half-pathetic, half-cynical perception, he realized the fragility of innocence, and remembered how beauty and purity had betrayed him.

Always this one note possessed and obsessed him. Heine was constantly pulling himself up to check and disguise it, even in the midst of his singing. Then would come the inevitable reaction—the rush from one extreme to the other; from circumlocutory reticence to eager and complete explanation. Such outpourings of frank revelation occur almost regularly; they are placed like sign-posts at the beginning and end of all his sequences. He becomes distrustful of even his most direct symbols, and, apprehensive lest his readers may not understand all of him, he interrupts his series to plead, explain and almost to apologize for himself and his preoccupation with his sorrow. Such a realization is the reason for the lyric prologues to the "*Lyrisches Intermezzo*" and "*Die Heimkehr*" and the strange interruption of Number 43 in the latter series (*Werdet nur nicht ungeduldig*) with Heine's personal appeal for the reader's patience. . . . And then the thought of his lost beloved and her deception overwhelms him again! And back he runs to the dark chamber of his introspective gloom.

How constant was this thought of his betrayal, his eternal 'brooding on the addled eggs of passion,' may best be seen by a perusal of "*Die Heimkehr.*" As in the "*Lyrisches Intermezzo,*" so here he rings the changes on the one theme—with very few changes.

But a new poignancy enters; a sharper lyricism caused by Heine's attempts to forget his sadness, and the realization of his inability to do so. Early in 1822, at the age of twenty-three, Heine had published his 'Lyrical Intermezzo,' that burst of ineluctable beauty, in which he had poured his grief and, he hoped, had buried it. A year later he went to Hamburg, the city which he hated, where he had loved and lost his Amalie; and although two years had passed since she had married, and although he had presumably written himself out of his old mood, the torments broke forth afresh. Every familiar street, every old acquaintance, every well-known turn, fascinated and tore him. Racked in soul and body (for his headaches were getting more and more acute) he went to Cuxhaven for a six weeks' stay, where the fresh salt winds of the North Sea temporarily soothed and the new environment inspired him. The outcome of all this was 'The Home-Coming,' with its shifting backgrounds of his "*verdammtes Hamburg*" and his beloved ocean. Time and again he shows in this cycle his effort to escape from the painful memories and the fresh bitterness awakened by his visit; he tries to forget himself in his passion for the sea or in brief and spasmodic love-affairs, but without success. After these brilliant interruptions, he is back at his old theme; despondent, tender, coarse, mocking, brutal, unforgiving—hugging always to his bosom the torture of his unhappy love.

IV.

In these translations I have endeavored, by the selections chosen, to show Heine's lyrical power not only at its best but at its most characteristic. For this reason I have included many poems usually glossed over by his translators; poems that are trivial enough in themselves, but necessary to the series that contains them, and necessary also to a complete appreciation of Heine's development. I have translated the 'Lyrical Intermezzo' in its entirety, and practically all of 'The Home-Coming,' the two cycles that represent the poet at his height. I have also included most of 'The North Sea' poems which, though not always lyric, have the sweep of the sea itself, a definitely musical surge that one finds in some of the best polyrhythmical lines of Whitman and the unrhymed 'voluntaries' of Henley. Instead of "approaching perilously near ungainly prose" (John Todhunter's incredible dictum) these precursors of modern *vers-libre* have the sonorous dignity of blank verse blended with the sudden lift and music of a snatch of song.

To digress technically for a moment, possibly the English paraphraser's greatest difficulty in translating German poetry is the use of "*du*" and "*sie*." To use "thou" for "*du*" often gives a falsely old-fashioned and stilted ring to the entire poem, while "you" is likely to be abrupt and too colloquial. In Heine, the problem is complicated, for he himself often uses the more intimate personal pronoun ironically or, for certain wilful effects, archaically. I have ventured to employ both pronouns without any fixed program; using "thou" and "you" interchangeably wherever it seemed to fit the context and Heine's purpose best. We have in English no method of showing the shade of difference between the German two, and it is because of this (and incidentally because of an astonishing misconception of the poems themselves) that so many of Heine's translators have entirely missed the

point of several poems, which bear a piercing reminder
or a sarcasm subtler and more stinging than a column
of invectives. Examine the lyric Number 27 from
'The Home-Coming' beginning "*Die Jahre kommen
und gehen.*" The last quatrain runs:

> *Nur einmal möcht ich dich sehen,*
> *Und sinken vor dir aufs Knie;*
> *Und sterbend zu dir sprechen:*
> *"Madam, ich liebe sie!"*

"Madam, I love but you," Todhunter ineffectually
concludes. Even Mrs. Browning, possibly due to her
ignorance of German, rendered it, "Lady, I love but
thee." And another translator, surpassing them all in
incomprehension of the last line, turns Heine's bitterest
irony into maudlin sentiment. Thus Robert Levy:

> "Oh, that I once might see you,
>   Kneel to you! Then would I
> Say: '*Lady mine, I love you!*'
>   And speaking so, would die."

In this lyric, as in two or three others where Heine
depends on a pun for his satire, I have had to reconstruct the lines and use a phrase totally unlike the German to carry out a particular effect. This is also half
true of the almost baffling Number 30 in the 'Lyrical
Intermezzo.' Here Heine, in an effort to achieve a
light ironic emphasis, employs a series of French
derivatives with a single rhyme scheme. As embodying these intact would leave part of the verses untranslated, without even approximating Heine's purpose
(for the use of French is not, as it was with the Ger-

man writers, a superelegance of language), I have paraphrased them all, depending on a series of the same double rhymes for a similar half-satirical end.

As to the rhymes throughout the book, I have followed Heine exactly. With one or two exceptions, I have reproduced the masculine and feminine rhymes as they appear in the original. Certain effects of humor and speed are only possible this way. And, although the single rhyme is the more natural and frequent in English poetry while it is almost the reverse in German, I felt it imperative to preserve Heine's own form, both for the sake of the reader and in an attempt to echo some of the music. I regret that in many cases, particularly in the very simplest of the lyrics, that exquisite and fragile music has been broken. Many of his poems, while wholly colloquial in speech and casual and even trite in idea, are transmuted into magic by their word-music and the perfection of vowel and consonant sound. Such properties cannot be transplanted—the sense can be captured, the magic inevitably escapes. I would suggest that, having ascertained the meaning, the reader take up the German and read the original for the virgin beauty, the color and cadence of the melodic line. For the reader of German, even for one who has but a smattering of the tongue, this suggestion would be an impertinence. He already knows that Heine, unadulterated and undefiled, can only be had from Heine's own pages.

It is only in the hope of bringing the English reader closer to the source that these translations have been prepared. They furnish the key to the paradox of Heine; they are the words, if not the music to some of his immortal *opera*. And to instil in the listener an understanding of the masterpiece is the aim and hope of a libretto. It is a high purpose; and I will be proud if this version fulfils a part of it.

L. U.

*New York City,
July, 1916.*

NOTE: For all of the translations from "The Book of Songs" and "New Poems" I have used the editions of Carl Krabbe published in Stuttgart, as they seemed more complete and the individual cycles better arranged than in the subsequent and more sumptuous formats. For the balance of the poems *(The Romancero, The Lamentations, etc.)* I have used "Der Tempel" edition, published in Leipzig.

INTRODUCTION TO THE REVISED EDITION

The first edition of this volume could not have been published at a more inopportune moment. It appeared almost simultaneously with America's entry into the World War and, for a while, shared the patriotic hate which was lavished on everything connected with German culture—no matter how remote the era and no matter how antagonistic the dead creator may have been to the German politics of his period. Thus Wagner—who, because of his leadership in the political agitation preceding the revolution of 1848, was forced to leave Germany—was suddenly banished from our opera-houses; singers who attempted excerpts from his works were hissed from the concert-stage and, though the armistice was signed almost five years ago, the greatest of his music-dramas, *Götterdämmerung* and *Meistersinger,* needed a foreign Wagner Festival to revive them here in 1923. The public interest in poetry being less violent, there was considerably less outcry, though there were various protests when translations from the German appeared during the feverish hours of suspicion and spy-hunting. And yet the fact that Heine's bitter opposition to the Hohenzollerns compelled him to live in exile in Paris did not save his work from being wilfully misinterpreted. This misunderstanding is neither new nor surprising. But, as a rule, the process of distortion has been characteristic of Heine's translators rather than his critics. There is, in most of the Heine reproductions, a lack of

Introduction to the Revised Edition

something that is more fundamental than erudition or accuracy. This vital quality which is missing is not merely rhythmical ease, or verbal grace, or virtuosity, but a misapprehension, almost an ignorance, of the spirit behind the words. Or, instead of ignorance, let me say it is distaste. Not conscious repugnance exactly; but a desire not to see what seems to be vulgar or petty or painful in Heine, an effort to turn his rude laughter into refined badinage—in short, to prettify him into a pseudo-romantic, graceful and usually sentimental lyric poet. These interpreters attempt to appreciate the poems of Heine without appreciating Heine himself. And in their failure to approximate or even to want to understand the man, lies the secret of their failure to understand the poet and the poet's work.

This refusal to accept Heine as he was, with his mockery, his outspokenness, his bursts of coarseness and pain interrupting his most limpid and ethereal moments, is the reason why many of the versions are, even when they are fairly readable, scarcely reliable. Most of the translators have taken up the work in their best academic manner. They have approached Heine not only as pedagogs, but as pedagogs confronted with a talented, ill-behaved and generally inexplicable undergraduate. Here and there, a kindly professor has blinked an eye rather than witness an undignified prank; another has closed his ears to episodes too bitter or racy for the class-room. But the attitude has been almost always that of smiling, superior disapproval. Either they condemned Heine's own utterances with silence or negated them with corrective notes and explanatory apologies. Unable, by their soft and coddled traditions, to face the storm of Heine's mood—his wild

Introduction to the Revised Edition

mixture of naïveté and disillusion, of tenderness and brutality—they slurred over and devitalized whatever was too rude or untutored for their precise tastes. The result is the usual tasteless volume with nothing to remind one of the original but the bare design of a story, an occasionally brilliant line buried in banalities, a sense of something struggling beneath a weight of scholasticism, mawkish metaphors and a few hundred tortured inversions.

The present revised edition owes many of its changes to a friendly controversy with Professor Otto Heller and the excellent example of Howard Mumford Jones, whose version of *The North Sea* is remarkable for its triumphs over innumerable technical difficulties. I repeat, recognizing the great difference in tonal values of the two languages, that this English translation is little more than the " book of the opera," that Heine's music can only be heard in the original German. Heine's spirit, however, is somewhat less dependent on the felicities of tone and, if this writer's synthesis of Heine's peculiar philosophy in his own " Monolog from a Mattress " is a piece of poetic liberty, the present translator can claim not only a spiritual but a racial kinship with the most sentimentally sardonic of lyricists. The claim to such a kinship is advanced to give color to the writer's interpretation, not to avoid responsibility for the weaknesses in paraphrasing. There is no need for me to dwell on the inevitable lapses. To discover them, the reader will, unfortunately, not require my assistance.

L. U.

March, 1923.

MONOLOG FROM A MATTRESS

Heinrich Heine ætat 56, loquitur:

Can that be you, *la mouche?* Wait till I lift
This palsied eye-lid and make sure. . . . Ah, true.
Come in, dear fly, and pardon my delay
In thus existing; I can promise you
Next time you come you'll find no dying poet—
Without sufficient spleen to see me through,
The joke becomes too tedious a jest.
I am afraid my mind is dull to-day;
I have that—something—heavier on my chest
And then, you see, I've been exchanging thoughts
With Doctor Franz. He talked of Kant and Hegel
As though he'd nursed them both through whooping
    cough
And, as he left, he let his finger shake
Too playfully, as though to say, " Now off
With that long face—you've years and years to live."
I think he thinks so. But, for Heaven's sake,
Don't credit it—and never tell Mathilde.
Poor dear, she has enough to bear already. . . .

This *was* a month! During my lonely weeks
One person actually climbed the stairs
To seek a cripple. It was Berlioz—
But Berlioz always was original.
Meissner was also here; he caught me unawares,
Scribbling to my old mother. " What! " he cried,
" Is the old lady of the *Dammthor* still alive?
And do you write her still? " " Each month or so."

Monolog from a Mattress

"And is she not unhappy then, to find
How wretched you must be?" "How can she
    know?
You see," I laughed, "she thinks I am as well
As when she saw me last. She is too blind
To read the papers—some one else must tell
What's in my letters, merely signed by me.
Thus she is happy. For the rest—
That any son should be as sick as I,
No mother could believe."
                 Ja, so it goes.

Come here, my lotus-flower. It is best
I drop the mask to-day; the half-cracked shield
Of mockery calls for younger hands to wield.
Laugh—or I'll hug it closer to my breast.
So . . . I can be as mawkish as I choose
And give my thoughts an airing, let them loose
For one last rambling stroll before— Now look!
Why tears? You never heard me say "the end."
Before . . . before I clap them in a book
And so get rid of them once and for all.
This is their holiday—we'll let them run—
Some have escaped already. There goes one . . .
What, I have often mused, did Goethe mean?
So many years ago at Weimar, Goethe said
"Heine has all the poet's gifts but love."
Good God! But that is all I ever had.
More than enough! So much of love to give
That no one gave me any in return.
And so I flashed and snapped in my own fires
Until I stood, with nothing left to burn,
A twisted trunk, in chilly isolation.
Ein Fichtenbaum steht einsam—you recall?

Monolog from a Mattress

I was that Northern tree and, in the South,
Amalia . . . So I turned to scornful cries,
Hot iron songs to save the rest of me;
Plunging the brand in my own misery.
Crouching behind my pointed wall of words,
Ramparts I built of moons and loreleys,
Enchanted roses, sphinxes, love-sick birds,
Giants, dead lads who left their graves to dance,
Fairies and phœnixes and friendly gods—
A curious frieze, half Renaissance, half Greek,
Behind which, in revulsion of romance,
I lay and laughed—and wept—till I was weak.
Words were my shelter, words my one escape.
Words were my weapons against everything.
Was I not once the son of Revolution?
Give me the lyre, I said, and let me sing
My song of battle: Words like furious stars
Shot down with power to burn the palaces;
Words like bright javelins to fly with fierce
Hate of the oily Philistines and glide
Through all the seven heavens till they pierce
The pious hypocrites who dare to creep
Into the Holy Places. "Then," I cried,
" I am a fire to rend and roar and leap;
I am all joy and song, all sword and flame!"
Ha—you observe me passionate. I aim
To curb these wild emotions lest they soar
Or drive against my will. (So I have said
These many years—and still they are not tame.)
Scraps of a song keep rumbling in my head . . .
Listen—you never heard me sing before.

Monolog from a Mattress

When a false world betrays your trust
    And stamps upon your fire,
When what seemed blood is only rust,
    Take up the lyre!

How quickly the heroic mood
    Responds to its own ringing;
The scornful heart, the angry blood
    Leap upward, singing!

Ah, that was how it used to be. But now,
Du schöner Todesengel, it is odd
How more than calm I am. Franz said it shows
Power of religion, and it does, perhaps—
Religion or morphine or poultices—God knows.
I sometimes have a sentimental lapse
And long for saviours and a physical God.
When health is all used up, when money goes,
When courage cracks and leaves a shattered will,
Then Christianity begins. For a sick Jew,
It is a very good religion . . . Still,
I fear that I will die as I have lived,
A long-nosed heathen playing with his scars,
A pagan killed by weltschmerz . . . I remember,
Once when I stood with Hegel at a window,
I, being full of bubbling youth and coffee,
Spoke in symbolic tropes about the stars.
Something I said about " those high
Abodes of all the blest " provoked his temper.
" Abodes? The stars? " He froze me with a sneer,
" A light eruption on the firmament."
" But," cried romantic I, " is there no sphere
Where virtue is rewarded when we die? "
And Hegel mocked, " A very pleasant whim.

Monolog from a Mattress

So you demand a bonus since you spent
One lifetime and refrained from poisoning
Your testy grandmother!" . . . How much of him
Remains in me—even when I am caught
In dreams of death and immortality.

To be eternal—what a brilliant thought!
It must have been conceived and coddled first
By some old shopkeeper in Nuremberg,
His slippers warm, his children amply nursed,
Who, with his lighted meerschaum in his hand,
His nightcap on his head, one summer night
Sat drowsing at his door. And mused, how grand
If all of this could last beyond a doubt—
This well-fed moon, this plump *gemüthlichkeit;*
Pipe, breath and summer never going out—
To vegetate through all eternity . . .
But no such everlastingness for me!
God, if he can, keep me from such a blight.

> *Death, it is but the long, cool night,*
> *And Life's a dull and sultry day.*
> *It darkens; I grow drowsy;*
> *I am weary of the light.*

> *Over my bed a strange tree gleams*
> *And there a nightingale is loud.*
> *She sings of love, love only . . .*
> *I hear it, even in dreams.*

My Mouche, the other day as I lay here,
Slightly propped up upon this mattress-grave
In which I've been interred these few eight years,
I saw a dog, a little pampered slave,

Monolog from a Mattress

Running about and barking. I would have given
Heaven could I have been that dog; to thrive
Like him, so senseless—and so much alive!
And once I called myself a blithe Hellene,
Who am too much in love with life to live.
(The shrug is pure Hebraic) . . . For what I've been,
A lenient Lord will tax me—and forgive.
Dieu me pardonnera—c'est son métier.
But this is jesting. There are other scandals
You haven't heard. . . . Can it be dusk so soon?
Or is this deeper darkness . . .? Is that you,
Mother? How did you come? Where are the candles? . . .
Over my bed a strange tree gleams—half filled
With stars and birds whose white notes glimmer through
Its seven branches now that all is stilled.
What? Friday night again and all my songs
Forgotten? Wait . . . I still can sing—
Sh'ma Yisroel Adonai Elohenu,
Adonai Echod . . .
          Mouche . . . Mathilde! . . .

LOUIS UNTERMEYER.

CONTENTS

	PAGE
PREFACE	v

BOOK OF SONGS

Preface to the Third Edition of *Buch der Lieder* . . . 3

YOUNG SORROWS

I dreamt I saw a dwarf in dapper clothing *Im Traum sah ich ein Männchen, klein und putzig* .	9
Why is my mad blood rushing so? *Was treibt und tobt mein tolles Blut?*	9
I came from my true love's house and stood *Ich kam von meiner Herrin Haus*	11
I lay and slept, and slept right well *Ich lag und schlief, und schlief recht mild*	17

SONGS

When I am with my own adored *Wenn ich bei meiner Liebsten bin*	21
Mornings I arise and wonder *Morgens steh' ich auf und frage*	21
It drives me here, it drives me there *Es treibt mich hin, es treibt mich her!*	21
I wandered under the branches *Ich wandelte unter den Bäumen*	22
Beloved, lay your hand on my heart in its gloom *Lieb Liebchen, leg's Händchen aufs Herze mein* . .	23
I wish that all my love-songs *Ich wollte, meine Lieder*	23
Lovely cradle of my sorrow *Schöne Wiege meiner Leiden*	24
Hill and hall are mirrored brightly *Berg' und Burgen schaun herunter*	25
I despaired at first, declaring *Anfangs wollt' ich fast verzagen*	25
When young hearts break with passion *Wenn junge Herzen brechen*	26

xxvi   Contents

	PAGE
There's green on the meadow and river *Die Wälder und Felder grünen*	26
I shall go and walk in the woods a space *Ich will mich im grünen Wald ergehn*	27
That I must love you, Mopser *Dass ich dich liebe, o Möpschen*	27
THE NUPTIAL EVE *Zum Polterabend*	28

ROMANCES

THE MOUNTAIN ECHO *Die Bergstimme*	33
POOR PETER *Der arme Peter*	34
THE GRENADIERS *Die Grenadiere*	35
THE MESSAGE *Die Botschaft*	37
THE MINNESINGERS *Die Minnesänger*	38
THE WOUNDED KNIGHT *Der wunde Ritter*	39
THE LESSON *Die Lehre*	39
ABSOLUTELY! *Wahrhaftig!*	40

LYRICAL INTERMEZZO

All my anguish, all my rages *Meine Qual und meine Klagen*	43
PROLOG *Es war mal ein Ritter, trübselig und stumm*	43
1. 'Twas in the magic month of May *Im wunderschönen Monat Mai*	45
2. Out of my tears and sorrows *Aus meinen Thränen spriessen*	45
3. The rose and the lily, the dove and the sun *Die Rose, die Lilje, die Taube, die Sonne*	46
4. Whene'er I gaze into thine eyes *Wenn ich in deine Augen seh'*	46
5. Your face so sweet and fair, it seems *Dein Angesicht, so lieb und schön*	46

Contents   xxvii

		PAGE
6.	Oh lean thy cheek upon my cheek *Lehn' deine Wang' an meine Wang'*	47
7.	I will baptize my spirit *Ich will meine Seele tauchen*	47
8.	Immovable for ages *Es stehen unbeweglich*	47
9.	On the wings of Song, my dearest, *Auf Flügeln des Gesanges*	48
10.	The lotus-flower cowers *Die Lotosblume ängstigt*	49
11.	In the Rhine, that stream of wonder *Im Rhein, im schönen Strome*	49
12.	You love me not—you love me not *Du liebst mich nicht, du liebst mich nicht* . .	50
13.	O come, love—now I resign me *Du sollst mich liebend umschliessen* . . .	50
14.	O kiss me, love, and never swear *O schwöre nicht und küsse nur* . . .	51
15.	Upon my dearest's little eyes *Auf meiner Herzliebsten Äugelein* . . .	51
16.	The world is dull, the world is blind *Die Welt ist dumm, die Welt ist blind* . .	52
17.	Come, and you shall tell me, dearest *Liebste, sollst mir heute sagen:* . . .	52
18.	Like the Foam-born, my love glows in *Wie die Wellenschaumgeborene* . . .	53
19.	I will not mourn altho' my heart be torn *Ich grolle nicht, und wenn das Herz auch bricht* .	53
20.	Yes, thou art wretched, and I do not mourn *Ja, du bist elend, und ich grolle nicht* . .	54
21.	Oh what a piping and shrilling *Das ist ein Flöten und Geigen* . . .	54
22.	So now you have forgotten wholly *So hast du ganz und gar vergessen* . . .	55
23.	And were it made known to the flowers *Und wüssten's die Blumen, die kleinen* . .	55
24.	Oh why are all the roses so pale *Warum sind denn die Rosen so blass* . . .	56
25.	They have told you many stories *Sie haben dir viel erzählet*	56
26.	The linden bloomed and the nightingale sang *Die Linde blühte, die Nachtigall sang* . .	57
27.	How deep we were wrapped in each other's life *Wir haben viel für einander gefühlt* . .	58

Contents

xxviii

		PAGE
28.	I have no faith in Heaven *Ich glaub' nicht an den Himmel*	58
29.	You were steadfast and true the longest *Du bleibest mir treu am längsten*	59
30.	The earth kept hoarding up its treasure *Die Erde war so lange geizig*	59
31.	And thus, as I wasted so many a day *Und als ich so lange, so lange gesäumt*	60
32.	The violets blue which are her eyes *Die blauen Veilchen der Äugelein*	60
33.	The world is so fair and the heavens so blue *Die Welt ist so schön und der Himmel so blau*	60
34.	Love, when you sink where darkness lies *Mein süsses Lieb, wenn du im Grab*	61
35.	A pine tree stands so lonely *Ein Fichtenbaum steht einsam*	61
36.	Stars, with fair and golden ray *Schöne, helle, goldne Sterne*	62
37.	Oh were I but the stool that she *Ach, wenn ich nur der Schemel wär'*	62
38.	Since my love and I did part *Seit die Liebste war entfernt*	63
39.	From grief too great to banish *Aus meinen grossen Schmerzen*	63
40.	It will not die, but solely *Ich kann es nicht vergessen*	63
41.	Smug burghers and tradesmen are tripping *Philister in Sonntagsröcklein*	64
42.	From graves of times forgotten *Manch Bild vergessener Zeiten*	65
43.	A young man loves a maiden *Ein Jüngling liebt ein Mädchen*	66
44.	Friendship, Love, the Philosopher's stone *Freundschaft, Liebe, Stein der Weisen*	66
45.	I hear an echo singing *Hör' ich das Liedchen klingen*	66
46.	Now all of the flowers are gazing *Es schauen die Blumen alle*	67
47.	I dreamed of the daughter of a king *Mir träumte von einem Königskind*	67
48.	My dearest, we nestled devoted *Mein Liebchen, wir sassen beisammen*	68
49.	From ancient fairy-stories *Aus alten Märchen winkt es*	68

Contents   xxix

		PAGE
50.	I loved thee once—and I love thee now *Ich hab' dich geliebet und liebe dich noch!*	69
51.	On a radiant summer morning *Am leuchtenden Sommermorgen*	70
52.	My love and its dark magic *Es leuchtet meine Liebe*	70
53.	Many have made me wretched *Sie haben mich gequälet*	71
54.	The golden flame of Summer *Es liegt der heisse Sommer*	71
55.	When two who love are parted *Wenn zwei von einander scheiden*	72
56.	'Twas tea-time—the mildly esthetic *Sie sassen und tranken am Theetisch*	72
57.	My songs, they say, are poisoned *Vergiftet sind meine Lieder*	73
58.	Again the old dream came to me: *Mir träumte wieder der alte Traum*	73
59.	I stand on the mountain's summit *Ich steh' auf des Berges Spitze*	74
60.	My carriage rolls on slowly *Mein Wagen rollet langsam*	75
61.	I wept as I lay dreaming *Ich hab' im Traum geweinet*	75
62.	Beloved, in dreams we often meet *Allnächtlich im Traume seh' ich dich*	76
63.	A howling storm is brewing *Das ist ein Brausen und Heulen*	76
64.	Wild Autumn shakes the branches *Der Herbstwind rüttelt die Bäume*	77
65.	A star, a star is falling *Es fällt ein Stern herunter*	78
66.	The Dream-God led me to a castle grim *Der Traumgott bracht' mich in ein Riesenschloss*	78
67.	'Twas midnight, still and very cold *Die Mitternacht war kalt und stumm*	79
68.	They buried him at the cross-roads *Am Kreuzweg wird begraben*	80
69.	Now the night grows deeper, stronger *Wo ich bin, mich rings umdunkelt*	80
70.	Night lay upon my eyelids *Nacht lag auf meinen Augen*	80
71.	The songs, so old and bitter *Die alten bösen Lieder*	82

Contents

THE HOME-COMING

PAGE

1. In my life's enshrouded darkness
   In mein gar zu dunkles Leben 87
2. I do not know why this confronts me
   Ich weiss nicht, was soll es bedeuten 87
3. My heart is full of sorrow
   Mein Herz, mein Herz ist traurig 88
4. I pace the greenwood, bitter
   Im Walde wandl' ich und weine 89
5. The night is wet and stormy
   Die Nacht ist feucht und stürmisch 90
6. By chance I met on my journey
   Als ich auf der Reise zufällig 91
7. We sat at the hut of the fisher
   Wir sassen am Fischerhause 92
8. Oh lovely fishermaiden
   Du schönes Fischermädchen 93
9. The yellow moon has risen
   Der Mond ist aufgegangen 94
10. The moon is lying on the clouds
    Auf den Wolken ruht der Mond 94
11. Wrapped in clouds, as in a mantle
    Eingehüllt in graue Wolken 95
12. The wind pulls up his water-spouts
    Der Wind zieht seine Hosen an 96
13. The storm tunes up for dancing
    Der Sturm spielt auf zum Tanze 96
14. I pass your little window
    Wenn ich an deinem Hause 97
15. The vastness of the ocean shone
    Das Meer erglänzte weit hinaus 97
16. High up on yonder mountain
    Da droben auf jenem Berge 98
17. My sweetheart has a lily
    Die Lilje meiner Liebe 99
18. Wrapped in the distant sunset
    Am fernen Horizonte 99
19. Greetings to thee, oh city
    Sei mir gegrüsst, du grosse 100
20. The old paths and familiar streets
    So wandl' ich wieder den alten Weg . . . 101
21. I stood as in a spell
    Ich trat in jene Hallen 101

Contents

		PAGE
22.	The night is still; the streets are quiet *Still ist die Nacht, es ruhen die Gassen*	101
23.	How can you sleep so soundly *Wie kannst du ruhig schlafen*	102
24.	A maiden lies in her chamber *Die Jungfrau schläft in der Kammer*	103
25.	I stood bewildered, seeing *Ich stand in dunkeln Träumen*	104
26.	I, unfortunate Atlas! A whole world *Ich unglücksel'ger Atlas! eine Welt*	104
27.	The years keep coming and going *Die Jahre kommen und gehen*	105
28.	What means this lonely tear-drop *Was will die einsame Thräne*	105
29.	The pale, autumnal half-moon *Der bleiche, herbstliche Halbmond*	106
30.	Well, this is awful weather *Das ist ein schlechtes Wetter*	107
31.	They think that I am tortured *Man glaubt, dass ich mich gräme*	108
32.	Oh, your slim, white lily-fingers *Deine weissen Liljenfinger*	109
33.	"Has she never even shown you" *"Hat sie sich denn nie geäussert"*	109
34.	They loved one another, though neither *Sie liebten sich beide, doch keiner*	110
35.	When I told of my sorrows that wounded and tore *Und als ich euch meine Schmerzen geklagt*	110
36.	I called the devil and he came *Ich rief den Teufel und er kam*	111
37.	Mortal, mock not at the devil *Mensch, verspotte nicht den Teufel*	111
38.	My child, we once were children *Mein Kind, wir waren Kinder*	112
39.	My heart is crushed with grief, for sadly *Das Herz ist mir bedrückt, und sehnlich*	113
40.	As the moon through heavy cloud-drifts *Wie der Mond sich leuchtend dränget*	114
41.	I saw in a dream the Belovéd *Im Traum sah ich die Geliebte*	115
42.	Why, my friend, this same old fretting *Teurer Freund! Was soll es nützen*	116
43.	Listen; do not grow impatient *Werdet nur nicht ungeduldig*	116

		PAGE
44.	Now it is time that I should start *Nun ist es Zeit, dass ich mit Verstand*	117
45.	The good king Wiswamitra *Den König Wiswamitra*	117
46.	Heart, my heart, let naught o'ercome you *Herz, mein Herz, sei nicht beklommen*	118
47.	Child, you are like a flower *Du bist wie eine Blume*	118
48.	Child, I know 'twould be your ruin *Kind! es wäre dein Verderben*	119
49.	When I lie down for comfort *Wenn ich auf dem Lager liege*	119
50.	Girl whose mouth is red and laughing *Mädchen mit dem roten Mündchen*	120
51.	Snows and storms may whirl in torrents *Mag da draussen Schnee sich türmen*	120
52.	Did not my pallid face betray *Verriet mein blasses Angesicht*	121
53.	"Ah, my friend, you are in love" *"Teurer Freund, du bist verliebt"*	121
54.	I sought your side, the only *Ich wollte bei dir weilen*	122
55.	Sapphires are those eyes of yours *Saphire sind die Augen dein*	122
56.	I have lied to win you, precious *Habe mich mit Liebesreden*	123
57.	Life in this world is a muddled existence— *Zu fragmentarisch ist Welt und Leben*	124
58.	My head and brain are almost broken *Ich hab' mir lang den Kopf zerbrochen*	124
59.	They're having a party this evening *Sie haben heut Abend Gesellschaft*	124
60.	Oh, that I could capture my sadness *Ich wollt' meine Schmerzen ergössen*	125
61.	You've pearls and you've diamonds, my dearest *Du hast Diamanten und Perlen*	126
62.	He who, for the first time, loves *Wer zum erstenmale liebt*	126
63.	In your tepid soul and vapid *Zu der Lauheit und der Flauheit*	127
64.	Oh loveliest of ladies, may *O, mein gnädiges Fräulein, erlaubt*	127
65.	Of words and advice they were the donors *Gaben mir Rat und gute Lehren*	127

Contents   xxxiii

		PAGE
66.	This most amiable youngster *Diesen liebenswürd'gen Jüngling*	128
67.	I dreamt I was the dear Lord God *Mir träumt: ich bin dir liebe Gott*	129
68.	Torn from bright lips I loved; departing sadly *Von schönen Lippen fortgedrängt, getrieben*	131
69.	Alone in the dim post-wagon *Wir fuhren allein im dunkeln*	131
70.	Like a dark dream the houses *Wie dunkle Träume stehen*	132
71.	With kisses my lips were wounded by you *Hast du die Lippen mir wund geküsst*	133
72.	And when you're once my wedded wife *Und bist du erst mein ehlich Weib*	133
73.	When I am enwrapped in her tender embraces *Als sie mich umschlang mit zärtlichem Pressen*	134
74.	Oh what lies there are in kisses! *In den Küssen, welche Lüge*	134
75.	Upon your snow-white shoulder *An deine schneeweisse Schulter*	135
76.	The blue Hussars go bugling *Es blasen die blauen Husaren*	135
77.	In my youth when Love was yearning *Habe auch in jungen Jahren*	136
78.	Have you really grown to hate me? *Bist du wirklich mir so feindlich*	136
79.	Ah, those eyes again which always *Ach, die Augen sind es wieder*	137
80.	'Tis a heavenly pleasure indeed *Himmlisch war's, wenn ich bezwang*	137
81.	Hard to understand your gabble *Selten habt ihr mich verstanden*	138
82.	And still the eunuchs grumbled *Doch die Kastraten klagten*	138
83.	On the walls of Salamanca *Auf den Wällen Salamankas*	139
84.	As soon as we met we were 'wrapped in each other *Kaum sahen wir uns, und an Augen und Stimmen*	139
85.	Over the mountains the sun throws his fire *Über die Berge steigt schon die Sonne*	140
86.	In Halle's market-place *Zu Halle auf dem Markt*	140
87.	Lovely and efficient lady *Schöne, wirtschaftliche Dame*	141

Contents

		PAGE
88.	Softly now the summer twilight *Dämmernd liegt der Sommerabend*	141
89.	Night lies on the strange, dark roadways *Nacht liegt auf den fremden Wegen*	142
90.	Death—it is but the long, cool night *Der Tod, das ist die kühle Nacht*	142
91.	"Where is now your precious darling" *"Sag, wo ist dein schönes Liebchen"*	143

DUSK OF THE GODS
  Gotterdämmerung 143

DONNA CLARA
  Donna Clara 146

THE PILGRIMAGE TO KEVLAAR
  Die Wallfahrt nach Kevlaar 150

THE HARZ JOURNEY

PROLOG
  Prolog 157

A MOUNTAIN IDYL
  Berg-Idylle 158

THE HERD-BOY
  Der Hirtenknabe 166

ON THE BROCKEN
  Auf dem Brocken 167

THE ILSE
  Die Ilse 168

THE NORTH SEA—FIRST CYCLE

CORONATION
  Krönung 173

TWILIGHT
  Abenddämmerung 174

NIGHT ON THE STRAND
  Die Nacht am Strande 175

POSEIDON
  Poseidon 178

DECLARATION
  Erklärung 180

A NIGHT IN THE CABIN
  Nachts in der Kajüte 181

STORM
  Sturm 181

Contents

	PAGE
CALM AT SEA *Meeresstille*	183
PEACE *Frieden*	184

THE NORTH SEA—SECOND CYCLE

SEA GREETING *Meergruss*	187
SUNSET *Untergang der Sonne*	189
THE GODS OF GREECE *Die Götter Griechenlands*	191
QUESTIONS *Fragen*	194
THE PHOENIX *Der Phönix*	195
SEA-SICKNESS *Seekrankheit*	196
EPILOG *Epilog*	199

NEW POEMS

NEW SPRING

1. Now the wood blooms like a maiden
   In dem Walde spriesst und grünt es 205
2. Lightly swinging bells are ringing
   Leise zieht durch mein Gemüt 205
3. The butterfly is in love with the rose
   Der Schmetterling ist in die Rose verliebt . . 206
4. All the trees are full of music
   Es erklingen alle Bäume 206
5. "In the beginning was the Word"
   Im Anfang war die Nachtigall 207
6. I must go forth, the bells are pealing
   Es drängt die Not, es läuten die Glocken . . . 208
7. The deep, blue eyes of Springtime
   Die blauen Frühlingsaugen 208
8. The slender water-lily
   Die schlanke Wasserlilie 209

Contents

		PAGE
9.	Your eyes' blue depths are lifted *Mit deinen blauen Augen*	209
10.	The rose is fragrant—but can she be feeling *Die Rose duftet—doch ob sie empfindet*	210
11.	As the moon's pale image trembles *Wie die Mondes Abbild zittert*	210
12.	Our hearts have made a holy *Es haben unsre Herzen*	210
13.	Kisses that one steals in darkness *Küsse, die man stiehlt im Dunkeln*	211
14.	There was an aged monarch *Es war ein alter König*	211
15.	In memory many pictures *In meiner Erinnrung erblühen*	212
16.	Every day I send you violets *Morgens send' ich dir die Veilchen*	212
17.	Your letter does not move me *Der Brief, den du geschrieben*	213
18.	Do not fear that I'll betray my *Sorge nie, dass ich verrate*	213
19.	Stars with golden feet are walking *Sterne mit den goldnen Füsschen*	214
20.	The sweet desires blossom *Die holden Wünsche blühen*	214

A MISCELLANY

SERAPHINE

1.	Night has come with silent footsteps *An dem stillen Meeresstrande*	217
2.	I was aware you loved me *Dass du mich liebst, das wusst' ich*	217
3.	Upon these rocks we shall erect *Auf diesen Felsen bauen wir*	218
4.	Shadow-love and shadow-kisses *Schattenküsse, Schattenliebe*	219
5.	Upon the shore, a maiden *Das Fräulein stand am Meere*	219
6.	With great, black sails my ship sails on *Mit schwarzen Segeln segelt mein Schiff*	219
7.	I've told no man how shameful *Wie schändlich du gehandelt*	220
8.	The waves draw in and stumble *Es ziehen die brausenden Wellen*	220

Contents　　　　　　　　　xxxvii

	PAGE
9. The runic stone juts into the sea 　　*Es ragt ins Meer der Runenstein*	221
10. The sea is sparkling in the sun 　　*Das Meer erstrahlt im Sonnenschein* . . .	221

ANGÉLIQUE

1. Although you hurried coldly past me 　　*Wie rasch du auch vorüberschrittest* . .	222
2. How from such a chance beginning 　　*Wie entwickeln sich doch schnelle* . . .	222
3. Ah, how sweet you are, confiding 　　*Ach, wie schön bist du, wenn traulich* . .	223
4. I close her eyes, and keep them tight 　　*Ich halte ihr die Augen zu*	224
5. When in your arms and in our kisses 　　*Wenn ich, beseligt vom schönen Küssen* . .	224
6. Do not fear, my love; no danger 　　*Fürchte nichts, geliebte Seele* . . .	225
7. Don't send me off, now that your thirst 　　*Schaff mich nicht ab, wenn auch den Durst* .	225
8. This mad carnival of loving 　　*Dieser Liebe toller Fasching*	226

HORTENSE

1. We stood upon the corner, where 　　*Wir standen an der Strasseneck* . . .	227
2. In all my dreams by daylight 　　*In meinen Tagesträumen*	227
3. Deep within a lovely garden 　　*Steht ein Baum im schönen Garten* . .	228
4. The words you keep repeating 　　*Nicht lange täuschte mich das Glück* . .	228

YOLANDA AND MARIE

1. Which of them shall I fall in love with? 　　*In welche soll ich mich verlieben* . . .	229
2. Flowers on your breast—I heed 'em! 　　*Vor der Brust die trikoloren*	229
3. Youth is leaving me; but daily 　　*Jugend, die mir täglich schwindet* . .	230

EMMA

1. He stands as stark as a tree-trunk 　　*Er steht so starr wie ein Baumstamm* . .	230
2. Emma, tell me, tell me truly: 　　*Emma, sage mir die Wahrheit* . . .	231
3. Now with shadows, dull and dreary 　　*Schon mit ihren schlimmsten Schatten* . .	231

Contents

CATHERINE
1. A lovely star has risen in my night
   Ein schöner Stern geht auf in meiner Nacht . 232
2. You lie in my arms so gladly
   Du liegst mir so gern im Arme 232
3. I love this white and slender body
   Ich liebe solche weisse Glieder 233

KITTY
1. Eyes that I had long forgotten
   Augen, die ich längst vergessen 234
2. Your love for me (so says my pride)
   Mir redet ein die Eitelkeit 234
3. The sun is fair when it sinks in splendor
   Es glänzt so schön die sinkende Sonne . . 235
4. Her letter leaves me breathless—
   Er ist so herzbeweglich 235
5. Swift as a deer, my bark
   Es läuft dahin die Barke 236
6. The joy that kissed me yesterday
   Das Glück, das gestern mich geküsst . . . 236

JENNY
My years now number five and thirty
Ich bin nun fünfunddreissig Jahr' alt . . . 237

ABROAD
1. "Oh this dear, delightful poet"
   O, des liebenswürd'gen Dichters 238
2. To-day you are so plunged in sorrow
   Du bist ja heut so grambefangen 239
3. I had, long since, a lovely Fatherland
   Ich hatte einst ein schönes Vaterland . . . 240

TRAGEDY
1. "Oh fly with me and be my love"
   Entflieh mit mir und sei mein Weib . . . 240
2. The hoar-frost fell on a night in Spring
   Es fiel ein Reif in der Frühlingsnacht . . . 241
3. Upon their grave a tree stands now
   Auf ihrem Grab da steht eine Linde . . . 241

BALLADS

A WOMAN
Ein Weib 245

SPRING FESTIVAL
Frühlingsfeier 245

Contents xxxix

	PAGE
THE ADJURATION *Die Beschwörung*	246
ANNO 1829 *Anno 1829*	247
PSYCHE *Psyche*	248
THE UNKOWN *Die Unbekannte*	249
AWAY! *Lass ab*	250
A MEETING *Begegnung*	251
THE FAITHLESS LOUISA *Die ungetreue Luise*	252

POEMS FOR THE TIMES

DOCTRINE *Doktrin*	257
A WARNING *Warnung*	257
DEGENERATION *Entartung*	258
HENRY *Heinrich*	259
TO GEORGE HERWEGH *An Georg Herwegh*	260
A TOPSY-TURVY WORLD *Verkehrte Welt*	260
GERMANY *Deutschland*	261
ONLY WAIT! *Wartet nur!*	262
THE WEAVERS *Der Weber*	263
FOUR SONGS	
Through my heart the most beguiling *Es erklingt wie Liebestöne*	264
Yellow roses as an offering— *Was bedeuten gelbe Rosen*	264
We laugh and we are troubled *Wir müssen zugleich uns betrüben*	264
It makes a man feel happy *Das macht den Menschen glücklich*	265

ROMANCERO

LAMENTATIONS, LAZARUS AND LAST POEMS

When all men have betrayed your trust
   Wenn man an dir Verrat geübt 269

PROLOG
   Prolog 269

THE ASRA
   Der Asra 269

FROM THE PRELUDE
   Präludium 270

FAREWELL
   Lebewohl 270

MYTHOLOGY
   Mythologie 271

SECURITY
   Solidität 272

AUTO-DA-FÉ
   Auto-da-fe 272

MORPHINE
   Morphine 273

SOLOMON
   Salomo 274

How slowly Time, the frightful snail
   Wie langsam kriechet sie dahin 274

Mediævalism's crudeness
   Mitteralterliche Roheit 275

EPILOG
   Epilog 276

WHERE?
   Wo? 277

ENFANT PERDU
   Enfant perdu 277

HYMN
   Hymnus 279

ALPHABETICAL INDEX OF FIRST LINES IN GERMAN . . . 281

BOOK OF SONGS

PREFACE TO THE THIRD EDITION
OF THE
"BOOK OF SONGS"

Das ist der alte Märchenwald

It is the old, enchanted wood;
  The linden-tree's in flower.
The cold, white magic of the moon
  Maddens me with its power. . . .

I wandered on, and as I went
  I heard the heavens ringing;
Of love and the keen ache of love
  The nightingale was singing.

Of love and the keen ache of love
  She sang; of tears and laughter—
So sad her mirth, so sweet her sobs,
  That dead dreams followed after.

I wandered on, and as I went
  A wide space lay before me.
And there, with towering spires, there rose
  A castle huge and stormy.

Barred were its windows; over all
  Lay grief and silence, giving
The sense that in these wasted walls
  Nothing but Death was living.

Before the door there lay a Sphinx,
  Half-horrible, half-human;
A lion's form in body and claws,
  The forehead and breast—a woman.

A woman fair! Her marble gaze
  Was sensuous and commanding.
Her dumb lips curved into a smile
  Of secret understanding.

The nightingale so sweetly sang,
  What use was my resistance—
I kissed her radiant face, and that
  Transformed my whole existence.

For lo, the marble statue woke;
  The stone was touched with fire;
She drank the fervor of my kiss
  With an unslaked desire.

She drank my very breath from me
  And then, with lustful ardor,
Her lion's claws sank in my flesh,
  Holding me closer, harder.

Oh exquisite torture, rapturous wounds!
  The pain and the pleasure unending—
For while I was thrilled with the kiss of her
    mouth,
  The claws were tearing and rending.

The nightingale sang " Oh wondrous Sphinx;
  Oh Love, why all this distressing
Mingling of death-like agony
  With every balm and blessing?

> "Oh lovely Sphinx! Explain to me
> This riddle that puzzles sages.
> I've pondered on it hopelessly,
> Alas, for many ages."

. . . .

—All this I could have said just as well in decent prose. . . . But when one reads over one's old poems, freshening a phrase here and there, and touching them up for a new printing, the lyric habit of rhyme and rhythm steals over one imperceptibly—and lo! it is with verse that I open this third edition of the "*Book of Songs.*"

Oh Phœbus Apollo! if these verses be bad thou wilt surely forgive me. . . . For thou art an all-wise god, and thou knowest well enough why it was that many years have passed since I have busied myself exclusively with the measuring and harmonizing of words. . . . Thou knowest why the flame which once delighted the world with its brilliant display of fireworks was suddenly turned to a more serious blaze. . . . Thou knowest why this silently glowing fire is now consuming my heart. Thou dost understand me, great and glorious god; for even so didst thou exchange, now and again, the golden lyre for the mighty bow and the death-dealing arrows. . . . Dost thou not still remember Marsyas, whom thou didst flay alive? That was long ago, and a similar example may be necessary. . . . Thou smilest, oh my eternal Father!

HEINRICH HEINE.

Written in Paris, February 20, 1839.

YOUNG SORROWS
(1817-1821)

Im Traum sah ich ein Männchen, klein und putzig

I dreamt I saw a dwarf in dapper clothing,
  Who walked on stilts, each step an ell or more.
  Sported white linen—but the stuff he wore
Was black inside: one saw the dirt with loathing.
Within he was all sham; a fuss and frothing
  To draw attention from the rotting core.
  He talked of being brave, and was a bore.
His courage was all cant, and came to nothing.

"And do you know that man, or can you guess?"
  The Dream-god asked me; and he showed me then
  A picture of a church. . . . And of all men
The dwarf was at the altar, nothing less,
My love beside him; both were saying "Yes!"
  And twice a thousand devils laughed "Amen!"

Was treibt und tobt mein tolles Blut?

Why is my mad blood rushing so?
Why is my heart in such a glow?
My blood speeds like an angry dart,
And seething fires consume my heart.

My blood is boiling, foaming, mad,
Because of an evil dream I've had. . . .
He came, the shadowy son of Night,
And bore me, gasping, in his flight.

9

He brought me to a brilliant house
Where harps and lights and gay carouse
And revelers raised a merry din.
I reached the hall; I entered in.

It was a wedding revelry;
The guests were seated smilingly.
And when the happy pair I spied—
Alas! My darling was the bride.

It was my love—the blushing bride!
A smiling stranger at her side.
I crept up close behind their chair
And silently I waited there.

The music grew; I stood quite still;
The happy clamor made me ill.
The bride, with ecstasy possessed,
Folded the bridegroom to her breast.

I saw the bridegroom fill his glass
And drink and with a gesture pass
The wine to her. She drank and laughed.—
And, woe! It was my blood they quaffed.

The bride then took an apple, and
Put it into the bridegroom's hand.
He took a knife and cut it straight.—
And, woe! It was my heart they ate.

Their looks were long, their glances blazed;
He held her lovingly embraced,
Kissing her hot cheeks passionately.—
And, woe! 'Twas Death's cold lips on me.

Young Sorrows

My tongue lay in my mouth like lead—
I could not speak, the words fell dead.
And then—the music through the hall,
The bridal couple leading all!

I stood there, lost to all the world;
The dancers round about me swirled.
His words grew warm, his whispers bold:
She reddened—but she did not scold. . . .

Ich kam von meiner Herrin Haus

I came from my true love's house and stood,
Wrapped in a dark and midnight mood,
Within a lonely churchyard where
The tombstones glistened bright and bare.

It was the glimmering moon that shone
Still brighter on the Minstrel's stone.
I heard, "Wait, brother,—the hour flies."
And, pale as the mist, I saw him rise.

It was the Minstrel, bone for bone,
Who rose and sat on his crumbling stone;
And he grasped his zither and sang this song
In a voice that was hollow and harsh and strong:

"Ha! do ye know the old refrain
Ye strings, that echoed with its pain?
Know ye the name thereof?
The angels call it Heaven's desire,
The devils call it Hell's own fire,
And man, he calls it—Love!"

Scarce had he shouted the final word
When all the buried people stirred.
Up from their graves they rose, and sprang
About the Minstrel as they sang:

"Love, oh Love, your power has led
Us to this, our final bed.
Eyes are closed in a quiet head—
Why do you call and rouse the dead?"

And loudly they rattled and whimpered and wailed,
They chattered and clattered and rumbled and railed;
And madly the swarm ran round and about
While the Minstrel played, and sang with a shout:

"Bravo! Bravo! Madmen still!
Welcome, madmen,
Good and bad men,
That my magic words could thrill!
Ye who lie, year in, year out,
In a dark and dusty drought,
Let this be a merry rout!
But look first
If there's any one about.
Fools we were when we were living,
While our burning blood was giving
Us a mad and passionate thirst.
Now, for pastime and for glory,
Every one shall tell his story;
Tell what brought him to this place;
    How he fared
    And was snared
In Love's mad and furious chase."

Young Sorrows

And then from the circle, as light as the wind,
There hopped a lean phantom who hummed as he grinned:

"A tailor's lad was I, sirs,
  (*With needle and with shears,*)
I was so slick and spry, sirs,
  (*With needle and with shears.*)
My master's daughter tricked me
  (*With needle and with shears,*)
And to the heart she pricked me
  (*With needle and with shears.*")

The spirits all laughed till their skeletons shook;
And a second stepped forth with a serious look:

"O, Rinaldo Rinaldini,
Robin Hood and Orlandini,
And Carl Moor (the best of those)
Were the models that I chose.

"I too, in a milder fashion,
Like these brigands, tasted passion;
While a certain lady's face
Haunted me from place to place.

"All my hopes were crushed and saddened;
And when Love at last grew maddened,
My mad fingers, growing rash,
Dipped into my neighbor's cash.

"But a watchman who was jealous
Said my mourning was too zealous;
Said I tried to dry my griefs
In my neighbor's handkerchiefs.

"Then the old policemen caught me;
To the station-house they brought me;
And the great, gray prison pressed
Me to its maternal breast.

"Thoughts of love (I could not choke 'em)
Plagued me still while picking oakum;
Till Rinaldo's shadow passed
And released my soul at last."

The spirits all laughed with a boisterous shout;
And powdered and perfumed, a third stepped out:

"As king of the boards I had striven
   To play every amorous rôle;
How often I ranted, 'Oh heaven!'
   And whispered a wild, 'Ah, my soul.'

"As Romeo none could do better;
   (My Juliet was always so fair!)
Though I acted my lines to the letter
   She never would answer my prayer.

"One night, as I started to stagger
   At the end, and as 'Juliet!' I cried,
I stuck the sharp point of the dagger
   A little too deep in my side."

The spirits all laughed with a boisterous shout;
And, clad in a white cloth, a fourth stepped out:

"The professor talked of the spirit and letter;
   He talked, and he talked—and I slept right well.
But one thing of his I enjoyed far better:
   His daughter, more lovely than words could tell.

"For me were her eyes and the smiles that she lavished,
  My flower of flowers, my Love's own light!
But my flower of flowers was stolen and ravished
  By a sour philistine, a wealthy old blight.

"Then I cursed all rich scoundrels and women together;
  The devil's own brew I prepared at the end.
Then drank with Lord Satan (two birds of a feather);
  He hiccuped '*Fiducit,* old Death is your friend.'"

The spirits all laughed with a boisterous shout;
And, a rope 'round his neck, a fifth stepped out:

"The Count, he boasted and bragged at his wine
Of his daughters divine and his jewel so fine.
Your jewel, dear Count, may be ever so fine,
But truly, I'd rather your daughter were mine.

"The Count kept them both under lock, bolt and key;
And a houseful of servants to guard them had he.
What mattered his locks and his servants to me—
I got me a ladder and mounted with glee.

"I stood at her window with ardor and joy,
When I heard a voice calling beneath me, 'Ho, boy!
Fine doings, my lad, but give me my share—
I'm also in love with the jewel that's there.'

"And thus the Count jeered at and mocked me, the while
His servants flocked 'round, with a sinister smile.
'The devil!' I cried, 'Do you think I would thieve?
I came for my love, which I'll take by your leave.' . . .

"But anger availed not, nor pleadings nor prayers;
And they marched in a solemn parade down the stairs.
When the sun rose, she started, astonished to see
The gallows so shining and heavy—with me."

The spirits all laughed in a boisterous shout;
With his head in his hand, a sixth stepped out:

"Love drove me to the poacher's trade,
And, musket on my arm, I strayed
Beneath the trees where ravens scoff
And croak and cough: 'Heads—off! Heads—off!'

"Oh, if I only saw a dove
I'd bring it home to my true love;
So I mused on, and every tree
Received my hunter's scrutiny.

"What do I hear? What billing's that?
Two turtle-doves! I've got 'em pat.
I crept up close; I caught the pair—
And lo! I found my own love there!

Young Sorrows

"It was my nestling dove, my bride;
A strange man snuggling at her side—
Now, you old marksman, aim, aim well!
There, in his blood, the stranger fell.

"Soon, through the woods, the hangman's crew,
With me, chief actor, in review
Passed the same trees where ravens scoff
And croak and cough: 'Heads—off! Heads—off.'"

The spirits all laughed in a boisterous chorus;
Until the Minstrel himself stepped before us:

"I once had a song that I cherished,
  But that sweet song is gone.
When the heart has loved and perished
  Then all of our singing is done."

And the crazy laughter grew twice as loud,
As the circle swayed wide with its ghostly crowd.
The bells struck "One" . . . and, to a man,
Howling into their graves they ran.

Ich lag und schlief, und schlief recht mild

I lay and slept, and slept right well,
  Free of the old despair;
When in my deepest dream there fell
  The vision, fond and fair.

Her face was like a marble girl's
  But lovelier with the change;
Her eyes had the cold sheen of pearls,
  And her bright hair was strange.

And softly, without stir or start,
  That maiden, marble-pale,
Came and lay down upon my heart,
  Mutely and marble-pale. . . .

I throb and thrill with hot unrest,
  The maddest fevers rise;
No throb nor thrill shakes her fair breast
  That is as cold as ice.

" No throb nor thrill can stir my breast
  That is as cold as ice.
Yet I know Love's eternal quest,
  Its pain and paradise.

" My mouth and heart's unwarmed with blood.
  No red stream courses through.
But do not shudder—think how good
  And kind I am to you."

She held me tight until the dawn,
  Struggling to no avail.
A cock crowed once . . . and she was gone,
  The maiden, marble-pale.

SONGS

Wenn ich bei meiner Liebsten bin

When I am with my own adored,
    Oh then my heart beats high;
I am as rich as any lord,
    The world is mine to buy!

But every time I leave her, then
    My wealth, that seemed secure,
Is spent—and I am once again
    The poorest of the poor.

Morgens steh' ich auf und frage

Mornings I arise and wonder
    Will she come to-day?
Evening passes, still I ponder,
    Still she stays away.

In the night with heavy cumber
    Sleeplessly I lie;
And half-dreaming, half in slumber,
    All my days go by.

Es treibt mich hin, es treibt mich her!

It drives me here, it drives me there;
    Soon, in an hour or two, I shall meet her,
    Yes, she herself, and what thing could be sweeter—
Heart of mine, why are you throbbing with care?

The hours are such a lazy lot!
  Creeping along with one foot dragging,
  Going the rounds, yawning and lagging—
Come, stir yourselves, you lazy-bones!

Now I am seized with the madness of speed.
  Oh, but they never were lovers, these hours;
  Banded together with hideous powers
They mock at the lover's unrest and his need.

Ich wandelte unter den Bäumen

I wandered under the branches
  Alone with my despair;
Touched with a host of memories
  I fell to dreaming there.

"Who taught you that word, oh, you songsters,
  You linnets that circle and soar?
Oh cease, for whenever I hear it
  My heart is afflicted once more."

"A girl came singing it always;
  From her own lips we heard,
And all of us birds recaptured
  That lovely, golden Word."

"Oh, how can you tell such a story,
  You birds, so sagacious and sly;
You also would capture my sorrows—
  But I will trust no one, not I."

Lieb Liebchen, leg's Händchen aufs Herze mein

Beloved, lay your hand on my heart in its gloom.
Do you hear that! Like tapping inside of a room?
A carpenter lives there. With malice and glee
He's building a coffin—a coffin for me.

He hammers and pounds with such fiendish delight
I never can sleep, neither daytime nor night.
Oh, carpenter, hurry the hours that creep;
Come, finish your labors—and then I can sleep.

Ich wollte, meine Lieder

I wish that all my love-songs
    Were flowers bright and rare;
I'd send them to my dearest
    And she might find them fair.

I wish that all my love-songs
    Were kisses that could speak;
I'd send them to my dearest
    To hang about her cheek.

I wish that these, my love-songs,
    Were peas, so firm and fat;
I'd make a nice, rich pea-soup—
    And she would relish *that!*

Schöne Wiege meiner Leiden

Lovely cradle of my sorrow,
   Lovely tomb where peace might dwell,
Smiling town, we part to-morrow;
   I must leave, and so farewell.

Farewell threshold, where still slowly
   Her belovèd footstep stirs;
Farewell to that hushed and holy
   Spot where first my eyes met hers.

Had you never caught or claimed me,
   Fairest, heart's elected queen,
Wretchedness would not have maimed me
   In its toils—as you have seen.

Never have you found me grieving
   For your heart with loud despair;
All I asked was quiet living,
   Quietly to breathe your air.

But you drove me forth with scourging,
   Bitter words and lashing scorn;
Madness in my soul is surging,
   And my heart is flayed and torn.

And I take my staff and stumble
   On a journey, far from brave;
Till my head droops and I tumble
   In some cool and kindly grave.

Berg' und Burgen schaun herunter

Hill and hall are mirrored brightly
  In the clear glass of the Rhine;
And my little ship sails lightly
  Where the sunlit waters shine.

Quietly I watch the shaken,
  Golden billows at their play;
And the thought still comes to waken
  What I hoped was laid away.

For the stream leaps to enamor
  With its warm and laughing light;
But I know, for all its glamor,
  Death is in its heart—and night.

Stream, you are her own reflection:
  She can also smile and sin;
She, like you, is all affection—
  Fair outside, and false within!

Anfangs wollt' ich fast verzagen

I despaired at first, declaring
  It could not be borne; and now—
Now I bear it, still despairing.
  Only never ask me how!

Wenn junge Herzen brechen

When young hearts break with passion
   The stars break into laughter,
They laugh and, in their fashion,
   Gossip a long time after:

" Poor souls, those mortals languish
   With Love; 'tis all they cherish.
It pays them back with anguish
   And pain until they perish.

" We never can discover
   This Love, so brief and breathless,
So fatal to each lover—
   And hence we stars are deathless.

Die Wälder und Felder grünen

There's green on the meadow and river;
   The lark seeks a loftier height;
And Spring has come in with a quiver
   Of perfume and color and light.

The lark's song has opened the prison
   Of winter-moods, stubborn and strong;
Yet out of my heart has arisen
   A fragment of sorrowful song.

The lark's all a-twitter and cheery:
   " Oh, what makes your singing so **drear?** "
The song is an old one, my dearie,
   I've sung it for many a year.

'Tis the same ballad, no other,
   With its burden of sorrowful rhymes—
Why, darling, your own grandmother
   Has heard it a score of times!

Ich will mich im grünen Wald ergehn

I shall go and walk in the woods a space,
Where flowers are gay and birds are singing;
For when I am once laid six feet under,
With eyes and ears that are closed to wonder,
I shall not see one flower lift its face
Nor hear one bird's song set the silence ringing.

Dass ich dich liebe, o Möpschen

That I must love you, Mopser,
   You surely understand;
For when I feed you sugar
   You always lick my hand.

You're nothing but a doggie
   And only pose as such.
All of my other friends, alas,
   Disguise themselves too much.

THE NUPTIAL EVE

1.

Mit deinen grossen allwissenden Augen

Yes, you are right. Your lingering glances
    Brim with a truth that makes me sad.
How could we two have met Life's chances—
    You are so good, and I so bad.

I am so bitter and malicious;
    Even my gifts bear wry respect
To you, who are so sweet and gracious
    And oh, so righteously correct.

2.

O, du kanntest Koch und Küche

Oh, you knew the cook and kitchen,
    Every turn and nook and bin;
In our childhood plays and struggles
    You would be the one to win.

Now you've won my own belovéd,
    That is droll; but, truth to tell,
This, my friend, is even droller:
    I must smile and wish you well!

3.

O, die Liebe macht uns selig

"Oh, 'tis Love that makes us grateful,
  Oh, 'tis Love that makes us rich!"
So sings man, and every fateful
  Echo bears his amorous speech.

You, you know the song's own spirit
  And its inner meaning, too;
Joyfully you wait and hear it
  Till the great day dawns for you.

Till the bride, with a caressing
  Smile is yours, from head to feet,
And her father gives his blessing—
  And a few things more concrete.

Linen, silver by the crateful,
  Silks with many a costly stitch. . . .
Oh, 'tis Love that makes us grateful,
  Oh, 'tis Love that makes us rich!

4.

Der weite Boden ist überzogen

The ground is carpeted with flowers,
  The woods are a triumphal arch;
And songsters in a thousand bowers
  Strike up a glad and welcoming march.

It is the Spring who enters, spreading
  Joy from his gay and sparkling eyes. . . .
You should have asked him to your wedding,
  For he goes gladly where true love lies!

ROMANCES

THE MOUNTAIN ECHO

Ein Reiter durch das Bergthal zieht

A horseman through a valley rode
　Singing a solemn stave:
" Am I nearer now to my true love's arms,
　Or am I nearer the grave?
　　There was no answer, save
　　" Nearer the grave."

And farther still the horseman rode,
　And a sigh broke from his breast:
" Though I must pass to my last abode,
　Perhaps the grave brings rest."
　　And echo half-expressed
　　" The grave brings rest."

The horseman wept a single tear
　And from his cheek it fell,
" And if in the grave there's rest for me
　Then all in the grave is well."
　　And echo rose to tell
　　" The grave is well."

POOR PETER

1.

Der Hans und die Grete tanzen herum

Oh Hansel and Gretel are dancing around,
There's shouting and clapping of hands there;
But Peter looks on with never a sound,
And, paler than chalk, he stands there.

For Hansel and Gretel are bridegroom and bride,
Around them the radiance lingers;
But Peter, in workaday clothes, turns aside;
He mutters, and bites his fingers.

Poor Peter still gazes; his grief is intense
And, watching the pair, he starts sighing:
"Oh were it not for my good, common sense
I'd end all my sorrows by dying." . . .

2.

"In meiner Brust, da sitzt ein Weh"

"Within my breast there's such a woe
   That I am torn asunder.
It stirs, and though I stay or go
   It drives me always yonder.

"It drives me to my love, it cries
   As though she still could heal me.
Alas, one look from Gretel's eyes
   And I must fly, conceal me.

Romances

"I climb the mountain's highest peak:
   Man is, at least, alone there;
Where all is still and none may seek
   My heart may weep and moan there."

3.

Der arme Peter wankt vorbei

Poor Peter, he goes stumbling by
As pale as lead, ashamed and shy.
And all the people stand and stare
Whenever Peter passes there.

The girls all whisper, "Give him room,
He must have risen from the tomb."
Ah no, my dears, your anguish save;
He's only going to his grave.

He's lost his love; his future's dim
And so the grave's the place for him.
For there his tortured spirit may
Await in peace the Judgment Day.

THE GRENADIERS

Nach Frankreich zogen zwei Grenadier'

Toward France there journeyed two grenadiers
   Who had been captured in Russia;
And they hung their heads and their eyes had tears
   As they came to the border of Prussia.

They heard the terrible news again
    That France had been lost and forsaken;
Her armies were beaten, her captains were slain,
    And the Emperor, the Emperor was taken!

Together they wept, these two grenadiers,
    To one thing their thoughts kept returning—
"Alas," cried one, half-choked with tears,
    "Once more my old wound is burning."

The other said, "The tale is told:
    I'd welcome Death about me,
But I've a wife and child to hold;
    What would they do without me?"

"What matters wife? What matters child?
    With far greater cares I am shaken;
Let them go and beg with hunger wild—
    My Emperor, my Emperor is taken!

"And this, oh friend, my only prayer
    When I am dying, grant me:
You'll carry my body to France and there
    In the sweet soil of France you'll plant me.

"The cross of honor with crimson band
    Lay on my heart to cheer me;
Then put my musket in my hand
    And strap my sabre near me.

"And so I will lie and listen and wait
    Like a sentinel, down in the grass there.
Till I hear the roar of the guns, and the great
    Thunder of hoofs as they pass there.

"And the Emperor will come, and his columns will
    wave;
  And the swords will be flashing and rending—
And I will arise, full-armed from the grave,
  My Emperor, my Emperor attending!"

THE MESSAGE

Mein Knecht! steh auf und sattle schnell

My page! arise and quickly mount
  The horse of swiftest stride;
And breathlessly, through wood and field,
  To Duncan's palace ride.

Wait softly in the stable there
  Until you are espied;
Then ask, "Which one of Duncan's girls
  Is going to be a bride?"

And if they say "The dark-haired one"
  Then rush home like the blast.
But if they say "The light-haired one"
  You need not ride so fast.

But in the village buy a rope,
  A rope with toughened strands.
Then ride back slowly, speak no word,
  And place it in my hands.

THE MINNESINGERS

Zu dem Wettgesange schreiten

Come the minnesingers, raising
   Dust and laughter and lament.
Here's a contest that's amazing;
   Here's a curious tournament.

Wild and ever restless Fancy
   Is the minnesinger's horse,
Art his shield, the Word his lance; he
   Bears them brightly round the course.

Many women pleased and pleasant,
   Smile and drop a flower down;
But the right one's never present
   With the rightful laurel-crown.

Other fighters nimbly canter
   To the lists, care-free and whole;
But we minnesingers enter
   With a death-wound in our soul.

And the one who wrings the inmost
   Song-blood from his burning breast,
He's the victor; he shall win most
   Praise and smiles and all the rest.

THE WOUNDED KNIGHT

Ich weiss eine alte Runde

I know an old, old story;
  Sad is the sound thereof:
A knight lies worn and wounded
  With grief for a faithless love.

He knows her faithless and scorns her
  Yet hangs on her wretchedly;
He knows his passion is shameful,
  Yet knows it is stronger than he.

He longs to ride to the tourney
  And shout with a challenging stir,
"Let him prepare for the death-blow
  Who finds a blemish in her!"

But well he knows there'd be silence
  From all save his own unrest;
And his own lance would have to be leveled
  At his loud and accusing breast.

THE LESSON

Mutter zum Bienelein

"Little bee, little bee,
Careful—stay close to me."
But what a bee should hear
Falls on a heedless ear.

Soon to the light he flies,
Deaf to his mother's cries
Calling him tremblingly:
"Little bee! Little bee!"

Blood of youth, never tame,
Seeks the eternal flame,
Where it burns fierce and free.
"Little bee—little bee."

Now with a mighty breath
Flame seeks a flaming death . . .
"Careful—beware of joy—
Oh, my boy! Little boy!"

ABSOLUTELY!

Wenn der Frühling kommt mit dem Sonnenschein

When the Spring comes in and the sun is bright
Then every small blossom beckons and blows;
When the moon on her shining journey goes
Then stars swim after her through the night.
When the singer looks into two clear eyes
Then something is stirred and sweet lyrics arise . . .
But flowers and stars and the songs just begun,
And moonbeams and eyes and the light of the sun,
No matter how much such stuff may please,
One can't keep living on things like these.

LYRICAL INTERMEZZO
(1822-1823)

LYRICAL INTERMEZZO

Meine Qual und meine Klagen

All my anguish, all my rages,
  I have poured and nought concealed here;
And, if you should turn these pages,
  You will find my heart revealed here.

PROLOG

Es war mal ein Ritter, trübselig und stumm

There once was a knight full of sorrow and doubt,
  With cheeks white as snow; indecision
Would cause him to totter and stagger about
  As though he were trailing a vision.
And he was so wooden, so awkward and dumb
That flowers and maidens, whene'er he would come,
  Would watch him and laugh in derision.

And often he'd sit in his gloom-shrouded place
  (From men and their joys he had broken)
And hold out his arms in a yearning embrace,
  Though never a word would be spoken . . .
But just as the hours to midnight now ran,
A marvelous singing and ringing began,
  With a knock at his door for a token.

And lo, his love enters—a zephyr that blows;
 Of shimmering sea-foam her dress is.
She glows till she grows like the bud of a rose,
 Her veil gleams with gems; and her tresses
Fall to her feet in a golden array;
Her eyes are impassioned. The lovers give way
 And yield to each other's caresses.

He holds her so close that his heart almost breaks.
 The wooden one now is afire;
The pallid one reddens, the dreamer awakes,
 The bashful is bold with desire.
But she, she coquettes and she teases, and then
With her magical veil she must blind him again,
 Who blindly does nought but admire.

In a watery palace of crystalline light
 She has 'witched him, and all that was bitter
Turns golden and fair, all is suddenly bright;
 His eyes are bemused with the glitter.
The nixie still presses him close to her side;
The knight is the bridegroom, the nixie the bride—
 Her maidens keep playing the zither.

Oh sweetly they sing and sweetly they play;
 Fair feet in the dances are shown there;
The knight in his ardor is swooning away
 And tighter he clasps her, his own there . . .
Then all in an instant is plunged into gloom,
And our hero is sitting once more in his room.
 In his poet's dim garret—alone there!

1.

Im wunderschönen Monat Mai

'Twas in the magic month of May
  When all the buds were springing,
My heart was filled with fervors,
  With dreams, and young Love clinging . . .

'Twas in the magic month of May
  When every bird was singing;
I poured out all the raptures
  With which my heart was ringing.

2.

Aus meinen Thränen spriessen

Out of my tears and sorrows
  The blossoming flowers arise,
And nightingales in choir
  Are born of all my sighs.

Dear girl, if you will love me
  Those flowers to you I'll bring—
And here before your window
  The nightingales will sing.

3.

Die Rose, die Lilje, die Taube, die Sonne

The rose and the lily, the dove and the sun,
I loved them all once—before Love had begun.
I love them no more. I worship now solely
The one and the only most holy and lowly.
She herself is the spirit of all these in one;
Being Rose and the Lily, the Dove and the Sun.

4.

Wenn ich in deine Augen seh'

Whene'er I look into your eyes
Then all my grief and sorrow flies;
And when I kiss your mouth, oh then
I am made well and strong again.

And when I lean upon your breast
My soul is soothed with godlike rest;
But when you swear, " I love but thee! "
Then I must weep—and bitterly.

5.

Dein Angesicht, so lieb und schön

Your face so sweet and fair, it seems
A vision only seen in dreams;
So seraph-like, so mild and frail,
And still so pale, so sadly pale.

Only your lips are red, and they
Soon kissed by Death turn cold and gray;
And dimmed will be the azure skies
That lie within those holy eyes.

Lyrical Intermezzo

6.

Lehn' deine Wang' an meine Wang'

Oh lean your cheek upon my cheek,
 Our tears thus shall mingle and flow, love!
And to my heart press close your heart,
 The flames beating so, love, shall glow, love!

And when the leaping radiance glows
 With tears like torrents thronging,
And when my arms are enfolding you close,
 I die of Love—and longing!

7.

Ich will meine Seele tauchen

I will baptize my spirit
 In the lily's glowing core;
The lily shall tremble and hear it—
 A song of the one I adore.

That song shall live and have me
 Thrilled with a subtle power,
Like the kiss that once she gave me
 In a sweet and poignant hour.

8.

Es stehen unbeweglich

Immovable for ages
 The stars are set above;
They look upon each other
 With all the pain of Love.

And oh, they speak a language,
  So wondrous, each to each,
That not the wisest scholar
  Can understand their speech.

But I have learned it, and never
  Can I hear it again unmoved;
For lo, I used as a grammar
  The face of my beloved!

9.

Auf Flügeln des Gesanges

On the wings of Song, my dearest,
  I will carry you off, and go
To where the Ganges is clearest;
  There is a haven I know.

In the moonlight's glow and glister
  Fair gardens radiate;
Eager to greet their sister
  The lotus-flowers wait.

Violets tease one another
  And gaze at the stars from the vales;
Roses are telling each other,
  Secretly, sweet-scented tales.

And lightly, trespassing slowly,
  Come the placid, timid gazelles;
Far in the distance, the holy
  River rises and swells.

Lyrical Intermezzo

O, that we two were by it!
   Beneath a palm by the stream.
To drink in love and quiet,
   And dream a peaceful dream.

10.

Die Lotosblume ängstigt

The lotus-flower cowers
   Under the sun's bright beams;
Humble and bowed with meekness
   She waits for the night among dreams.

The Moon, he is her lover,
   He wakes her with his gaze;
To him alone she uncovers
   The fair flower of her face.

She glows and grows more radiant,
   And gazes mutely above;
Breathing and weeping and trembling
   With love—and the pain of love.

11.

Im Rhein, im schönen Strome

In the Rhine, that stream of wonder,
   The great, the holy Cologne
Is mirrored, and there under
   The waves the Cathedral is shown.

The Cathedral has within it
  A portrait done in gold;
And, in my wild life's sin, it
  Has taken a wondrous hold.

'Mid flowers and angels she stands there
  Our Lady we bow before . . .
But the eyes and the lips and the hands there
  Are those of the one I adore!

12.

Du liebst mich nicht, du liebst mich nicht

You love me not—you love me not
  Oh that's a trivial thing, dear;
For when I see your face, my lot
  Is that of any king, dear.

You hate me, hate me—even this;
  Your red lips dare declare it!
Oh, let me have those lips to kiss
  And I, my child, can bear it.

13.

Du sollst mich liebend umschliessen

Oh come, love—now I resign me,
  I yield myself to your charms;
Oh come, that you may intertwine me
  With the tenderest, supplest of arms

    .   .   .   .   .

And winding thus and wounding,
   Embracing and crushing, is shown
The fairest of serpents surrounding
   The happiest Laocoon.

14.

O schwöre nicht und küsse nur

Oh kiss me, love, and never swear,
For women's oaths are light as air!
Your speech is sweet, but sweeter is
The silent answer in your kiss!
'Tis this alone that has my faith—
The word is but a perfumed breath.

. . . . .

Well, swear then, love; oh, swear away;
I will believe each word you say!
And as I sink upon your breast
I will believe that I am blessed;
I will believe your love of me
Stretches beyond Eternity.

15.

Auf meiner Herzliebsten Äugelein

Upon my dearest's little eyes
   I make the best *canzoni*.
Upon her mouth, so small in size,
   The best of *terza rima*.
Upon my darling's cheeks, likewise
   I make the loveliest stanzas . . .
And if she had a heart, upon it
I'd make a really charming sonnet.

16.

Die Welt ist dumm, die Welt ist blind

The world is dull, the world is blind.
  Each day more of a mad one!
It says, my dear, that, to its mind,
  Your character's a bad one.

The world is dull, the world is blind.
  Its dullness is really distressing;
It does not know how clinging and kind
  Are your kisses that burn with their blessing.

17.

Liebste, sollst mir heute sagen:

Come, and you shall tell me, dearest,
  Are you not a thing of dreams,
Such as, when the Summer's clearest,
  From the poet's fancy streams?

Ah, but no—a mien so mild, dear,
  Such a mouth and eyes that wait;
Such a loving, lovely child, dear,
  Not a poet could create.

Basilisks whose glances freeze or
  Hippogriffs and dragons dire;
Horrid, fabled things like these are
  Fashioned in the poet's fire.

But yourself and your pretenses,
   And those eyes that could not hate,—
And those false and fervent glances
   Not a poet could create.

18.

Wie die Wellenschaumgeborene

Like the Foam-born, my love glows in
   Splendor and her beauty's pride,
For she is the happy chosen
   One to be a stranger's bride.

Tho' this treason may be hard on
   Thee, my heart, thou patient one;
Bear it without sighs, and pardon
   What the pretty fool has done.

19.

Ich grolle nicht, und wenn das Herz auch bricht

I will not mourn altho' my heart be torn,
Oh love forever lost! I will not mourn.
Altho' arrayed in light and diamonds bright,
No single ray falls in thy heart's deep night.

I know this well. . . . I saw thee in a dream
And saw the night within thy heart supreme;
And saw the snake that gnawed upon thy
   heart . . .
I saw how wretched, oh my love, thou art.

20.

Ja, du bist elend, und ich grolle nicht

Yes, thou art wretched, and I do not mourn;
  Wretched, my love, it seems we both must be!
Until in death the weary heart is torn,
  Wretched, my love, it seems we both must be!

I see the scorn that on thy lips doth ride,
  I see the courage in thy flashing eye;
I see thy bosom heave with quenchless pride—
  Yet thou are wretched, wretched even as I.

Thy lips contract with unseen wounds and pain,
  And secret tears bedim the eyes I see;
Thy haughty bosom bears the hidden bane—
  Wretched, my love, it seems we both must be.

21.

Das ist ein Flöten und Geigen

Oh what a piping and shrilling;
  The trumpets blaze and blare,
To wedding-music thrilling
  My love is dancing there.

And with what a droning and groaning
  The drums and reeds are rent;
The while, with sobbing and moaning,
  The cherubim lament.

22.

So hast du ganz und gar vergessen

So now you have forgotten wholly
How once your heart was mine, mine solely;
Your heart had so sweet and so false a glow,
Nought could be sweeter or falser, I know.

So the love and the pain is forgotten wholly
That tortured my heart and made it lowly.
But whether the pain was as great as my love,
I know not. I know they were both great enough.

23.

Und wüssten's die Blumen, die kleinen

And were it made known to the flowers
  How wounded my heart must be,
Their tears would fall in showers
  To heal my agony.

If nightingale and linnet
  Knew of my sadness and pain,
Their singing would have in it
  A far more joyful strain.

If sorrow's tearful traces
  The golden stars could see,
They would come down from their places
  And try to comfort me.

But they cannot comprehend it—
One, only, knows my pain;
She took my heart to rend it
Again and yet again.

24.

Warum sind denn die Rosen so blass

Oh why are all the roses so pale,
  My love, come tell me why?
Oh why, with grasses once so hale,
  Do violets droop and die?

Oh why, to the sound of so doleful a lute,
  Do linnets lift their wings?
Oh why does there spring from each fragrant root
  The odor of dead things?

Oh why does the sun send so dreary a ray
  Over fields where he shone so brave?
Oh why is all of the earth as gray
  And desolate as a grave?

And I, myself, am so troubled and weak;
  My love, why should this be?
Answer my own; my lost darling, speak—
  Why have you done this to me?

25.

Sie haben dir viel erzählet

They have told you many stories
  And made a great to-do;
But why my spirit worries
  Has not been told to you.

They made a stir and pother,
   Complaining and shaking the head,
"A devil!" they said to each other;
   And you believed all they said.

And yet the very worst thing
   They never even have guessed;
For the worst and most accurst thing,
   I carry hid in my breast.

26.

Die Linde blühte, die Nachtigall sang

The linden bloomed and the nightingale sang,
   The great sun laughed with a friendly light;
You kissed me, my love, and the while my heart sprang,
   To your palpitant bosom you folded me tight.

The raven screamed harshly, the withered leaves fell,
   The sun's cold greeting was sharpened with spite;
We beckoned each other a frosty farewell,
   And politely you curtsied a curtsey polite.

27.

Wir haben viel für einander gefühlt

How deep we were wrapped in each other's life,
How well we behaved (and how bitter the moral);
How often we played at man and wife,
With never a blow or the sign of a quarrel.
We sported together in joy and in jest
And tenderly kissed and so sweetly caressed;
And finally playing like children that go
At hide and seek in the woodland together,
We managed to stray and to hide ourselves so
That each of us now is lost to the other.

28.

Ich glaub' nicht an den Himmel

I have no faith in Heaven
    Of which the preachers write;
Your eyes I do believe in,—
    They are my Heaven's light.

I have no faith in Godhead
    Of which the preachers read;
Your heart I do believe in,—
    No other God I need.

I have no faith in Satan,
    In Hell and Hell's fierce smart;
Your eyes I do believe in,—
    And in your wicked heart.

Lyrical Intermezzo

29.

Du bleibest mir treu am längsten

You were steadfast and true the longest;
   Your care you always gave me,
   Your thought would cheer and save me
When fear and need were strongest.

A gift of gold would not grieve you,
   And food you ne'er denied me;
   With linen you supplied me
Whene'er I had to leave you.

And for this great amount, He,
   The Lord, I pray will be tender
   To you and reward the splendor
Of your everlasting bounty.

30.

Die Erde war so lange geizig

The earth kept hoarding up its treasure;
   May spent it to a mighty babel
Of all that laughed and voiced its pleasure—
   But I, I find I am not able.

The bells' and flowers' speech reprove me,
   The birds converse as in the fable;
But all these wonders do not move me,
   For life is sad, and joy unstable.

Man bores me, even as the merest
   Gossip of friends about the table—
Because she is no longer "dearest,"
   But "Madam" . . . Hence my soul wears sable.

31.

Und als ich so lange, so lange gesäumt

And thus, as I wasted so many a day
In wandering and dreaming the hours away,
My love found the waiting too long a recess,
So she started to sew on her wedding-dress;
And she caught in her arms (oh deluded and duped)
As husband, the stupidest one of the stupid.

My loved one is so mild and fair
Her likeness haunts me everywhere;
The rose-cheeks and the violet-eyes
Year in, year out, their ghosts arise.
And that I should lose a love so dear,
Was the stupidest act of my stupid career.

32.

Die blauen Veilchen der Äugelein

The violets blue which are her eyes,
The crimson rose which her cheek outvies,
The lilies white which her hands disguise,
These blossom and glow; they never fade—
'Tis but the heart that has decayed.

33.

Die Welt ist so schön und der Himmel so blau

The world is so fair and the heavens so blue
And the breezes so mild that come whispering through,
And the flowers arise on the roadside anew,
And glisten and gleam in the morning dew,
And mankind is happy, whatever the view—
And yet I would lie in the grave uncherished
With naught but the ghost of a Love that has perished.

34.

Mein süsses Lieb, wenn du im Grab

Love, when you sink where darkness lies
   Before you and behind you,
I shall go down with all that dies
   And seek you out—and find you.

I'll clasp you with kisses, burning and wild,
   So pale, so unmoved and so cold there;
And trembling and weeping with ecstasy mild
   I will grow like a corpse and mold there . . .

The dead stand up as Midnight calls,
   They dance thro' airy spaces;
We two remain, wrapped in our palls.
   I lie in your embraces.

The dead stand up; the Judgment Day
   Calls them to pain or pleasure.
But we will dream the hours away
   Together at our leisure.

35.

Ein Fichtenbaum steht einsam

A pine tree stands so lonely
   In the North where the high winds blow,
He sleeps; and the whitest blanket
   Wraps him in ice and snow.

He dreams—dreams of a palm-tree
   That far in an Orient land,
Languishes, lonely and drooping,
   Upon the burning sand.

36.

Schöne, helle, goldne Sterne

Stars, with fair and golden ray,
Greet my loved one far away;
Say that I still wear the rue,
Sick at heart and pale—and true.

37.

Ach, wenn ich nur der Schemel wär'

(*The Head Speaks:*)
Oh were I but the stool that she
   Uses to rest her feet from pain;
Yea, tho' she stamped and trod on me,
   I would not murmur or complain.

(*The Heart Speaks:*)
Oh were I but the cushion too
   That holds the needle she employs;
Yea, tho' she pierced me through and
     through,
   Each stab would wake the wildest joys.

(*The Song Speaks:*)
Oh were I but the least—the mere
   Paper with which she curls her hair!
Then would I whisper in her ear
   What stirs in me, and all I dare.

38.

Seit die Liebste war entfernt

Since my love and I did part
Laughter died within my heart.
Many jesters quip and quaff;
But I cannot hope to laugh.

Since my love was lost to me
Weeping also ceased to be.
Broken, tortured, robbed of sleep—
But I cannot even weep.

39.

Aus meinen grossen Schmerzen

From my great grief, I fashion
  The little songs I utter;
  They lift bright wings and flutter
Off to her heart with passion.

Over her bosom they hover—
  But soon they fly homeward complaining;
  Complaining but never explaining
What, in her heart, they discover.

40.

Ich kann es nicht vergessen

It will not die, but solely
  This thought comes to condole,
How once I had you wholly;
  Your body and your soul.

Your body still I crave for,
  Your body's lovely growth.
Your soul you may dig a grave for,
  I've soul enough for us both!

I'll cut my own spirit in two, dear,
  And breathe in you half of the whole
And clasp you—thus forming anew, dear,
  One perfect body and soul.

41.

Philister in Sonntagsröcklein

Smug burghers and tradesmen are tripping
  Through woods in the smartest style;
Like goats they are hopping and skipping
  Admiring 'fair Nature' the while.

In eyes that are bleary and blinking
  A ray of Romance springs;
And great, long ears are drinking
  The song the sparrow sings.

But I am beclouding and shrouding
  My windows with curtains of gray;
For the ghosts of my fancies are crowding
  To pay me a visit to-day.

The old love comes in, creeping
  From Death's immense domain;
She sits by my side, and, weeping,
  She melts my heart again.

42.

Manch Bild vergessener Zeiten

From graves of times forgotten
   Old visions come to me
Revealing what, when near you,
   My life once used to be.

By day I wandered dreaming
   Through streets and alleys until
The people looked at me wondering;
   I was so moody and still.

By night 'twas somewhat better—
   The streets were an empty rout;
And I and my shadow together
   Went staggering blindly about.

With ever-echoing footsteps
   I crossed the bridge by chance;
The moon broke through the darkness
   And shot me an earnest glance.

I stood there, before your dwelling,
   And gazed into the night;
And gazed up at your window—
   My heart torn at the sight . . .

I know that, oft, from the window,
   Those lonely streets you scanned,
And saw me in the moonbeams,
   Like some white pillar stand.

43.

Ein Jüngling liebt ein Mädchen

A young man loves a maiden
  Whose heart for another has yearned;
This other loves another
  By whom his love is returned.

The maiden weds in anger
  The first good man she spies
Who runs into her pathway;
  The youth grows bitter and wise.

It is an old, old story
  But one that's always new;
And every time it happens
  It breaks a heart in two.

44.

Freundschaft, Liebe, Stein der Weisen

Friendship, Love, the Philosopher's stone,
These three things are ranked alone;
These I sought from sun to sun,
And I found—not even one!

45.

Hör' ich das Liedchen klingen

I hear an echo singing
  The song She sang for me;
And a fresh grief is wringing
  My heart's old agony.

A wild unrest is sweeping
  Me where the high woods grow;
There I shall lose, through weeping,
  My overburdening woe.

46.

Es schauen die Blumen alle

Now all of the flowers are gazing
  At the glowing and radiant sun,
And all of the brooks are seeking
  The heart of the sea as they run.

And all of the songs are flying
  To the most desired and dear—
Take with you my tears and my sorrows,
  Ye songs that are saddened and drear.

47.

Mir träumte von einem Königskind

I dreamed of the daughter of a king;
  With teary, weary faces
We sat beneath a linden's wing
  Wrapt in each other's embraces.

" I do not want thy father's throne,
  His scepter with gold o'erladen,
I do not want his brilliant crown,
  I want but thee, dear maiden."

"That cannot be," she said to me,
"For in the grave I am lying,
And only at night I come to thee,
Because my love is undying."

48.

Mein Liebchen, wir sassen beisammen

My dearest, we nestled devoted,
   Alone in a fairy-like bark.
The night was still; and we floated
   Out on the watery dark.

A Spirit-Isle we discovered
   In the moonlight's vague expanse;
Where airy music hovered
   And wove with a misty dance.

The sounds were sweet, and gladdened
   The night with their magicry.
But we—we passed it, saddened
   And worn on a widening sea.

49.

Aus alten Märchen winkt es

From ancient fairy-stories
   Beckons an airy hand;
A voice, with hints of glories,
   Sings of a magic land,

Lyrical Intermezzo 69

Where flowers have fairer blossoms
  In a golden evening's grace,
And bare their fragrant bosoms,
  Lifting a bridelike face.

Where all the trees are voicing
  Their songs, as in a choir;
Where rivers dance, rejoicing,
  And every wind's a lyre.

Where wilder passions quicken,
  Where wilder beauty throngs,
Till you are wonder-stricken
  With wonder-striking songs!

Ah, to be taken yonder
  To let my heart go free;
There in a land of wonder
  How blesséd it would be . . .

Ah, Land of Pleasant Places,
  Land of a dreamer's dream—
Alas, like foam it passes,
  Swept by a hurrying stream.

50.

Ich hab' dich geliebet und liebe dich noch!

I loved thee once—and I love thee now.
  Though the stars, in a golden shower,
Should fall . . . above the chaos and glow
  The flame of my love would tower!

51.

Am leuchtenden Sommermorgen

On a radiant summer morning
  Into the garden I come;
The flowers rustle and whisper
  But I—I wander, dumb.

The flowers whisper and murmur,
  Pleading as only they can:
"Oh be not wroth with our sister,
  Thou bitter and sorrowful man."

52.

Es leuchtet meine Liebe

My love and its dark magic
  Troubles me with its might,
Like a story, tender and tragic,
  Told on a summer night:

" In an enchanted bower
  Two lovers walk, half-awake;
The moon, like a great white flower,
  Lies on the breast of a lake.

" A picture: the maid almost pliant,
  And on his knees, the knight.
When lo, from the shadows a giant
  Springs,—and the maid takes flight.

Lyrical Intermezzo

" The knight sinks bleeding and dying,
   The giant tramps back to his hold " . . .
When in the grave I am lying
   The rest of the tale will be told.

53.

Sie haben mich gequälet

Many have made me wretched,
   Made mine an evil fate;
Some of them with their loving,
   Some of them with their hate.

My cup has been filled with poisons,
   They poisoned the bread I ate;
Some of them with their loving,
   Some of them with their hate.

Yet she, whose poison made me
   Wretched all men above,
Gave me no word of hatred,—
   And not a spark of love.

54.

Es liegt der heisse Sommer

The golden flame of Summer
   Burns in your glowing cheek;
But in your heart lies Winter,
   Barren and cold and bleak.

Soon it will change, my darling,
    Far sooner than you seek;
Your heart will harbor Summer,
    While Winter lines your cheek.

55.

Wenn zwei von einander scheiden

When two who love are parted,
    They talk, as friend to friend,
Clasp hands and weep a little,
    And sigh without an end.

We did not weep, my darling,
    Nor sigh "Why must this be . . ."
The tears, the sighs, the anguish
    Came later—and to me.

56.

Sie sassen und tranken am Theetisch

'Twas tea-time—the mildly esthetic
    Ensemble took '*Love*' as their theme;
The mood of the guests was 'poetic';
    They gushed like a lyrical stream.

"True love must be always platonic,"
    A hardened old councilor cried.
With a laugh that was almost ironic
    His wife looked upward and sighed.

A canon spoke, "We must resist 'em,
　These pleasures that rouse and harass,
Or else they will ruin the system."
　And a pretty young thing lisped, "Alas."

The countess, drooping and yearning,
　Said, "Love must sweep on like the sea!"
As, elegantly turning,
　She handed the baron his tea.

Still, it was not quite complete, dear—
　Your place stood empty above.
And oh, it would have been sweet, dear,
　To hear *you* prattle of love.

57.

Vergiftet sind meine Lieder

My songs, they say, are poisoned.
　How else, love, could it be?
Thou hast, with deadly magic,
　Poured poison into me.

My songs, they say, are poisoned.
　How else, then, could it be?
I carry a thousand serpents
　And, love, among them—thee!

58.

Mir träumte wieder der alte Traum

Again the old dream came to me:
　'Twas May; the world was vernal;
We sat beneath the linden tree
　And pledged a faith eternal.

Great love and a deathless oath we swore.
   And that I might ne'er forget it,
With a passionate kiss and a thousand more
   You took my hand—and bit it.

Oh sweetheart with the lips that cling,
   With eyes so clear and merry,
The oath was quite the proper thing—
   The bite, unnecessary!

59.

Ich steh' auf des Berges Spitze

I stand on the mountain's summit
   Emotional and absurd.
Sighing these maudlin verses:
   "Would that I were a bird!"

Oh if I were a swallow
   I'd fly to you for rest,
And, underneath your window,
   I'd build my little nest.

And if I were, oh dearest,
   A splendid nightingale,
All night you'd hear me singing
   From many a verdant vale.

And if I were a jay-bird
   My hopes to you I'd raise;
For you are kind to jay-birds
   And to the woes of jays![1]

---

[1] In this verse Heine puns satirically on the word *Gimpel*, which can mean either 'a bullfinch' or 'a fool.' Having no exact equivalent in English ornithology, I have been compelled to substitute another sort of bird.

60.

Mein Wagen rollet langsam

My carriage rolls on slowly;
   Woods are a cheerful green;
Valleys exult with flowers—
   The world's a magic scene!

I sit and think of my loved one,
   And dream that she might be here;
And lo, at my side three phantoms
   Curtsey and grin and leer.

They bow and they bob and they caper,
   Mocking, yet bashful and kind . . .
And then, like an eddy of vapor,
   They titter and pass with the wind.

61.

Ich hab' im Traum geweinet

I wept as I lay dreaming,
   I dreamed that you had died.
And, when I woke, the tear-drops
   Clung to my cheeks undried.

I wept as I lay dreaming,
   I dreamed you were false to me.
I woke, and for many hours
   Lay weeping bitterly.

I wept as I lay dreaming,
　　I dreamed that your love was true! . . .
I woke, to an endless weeping,
　　And the endless thought of you.

62.

Allnächtlich im Traume seh' ich dich

Beloved, in dreams we often meet,
　　And lo, your voice is kindly.
I fling myself at your gracious feet,
　　And weep there, long and blindly.

You shake your fair head, sunbeam-swept,
　　And oh, that look appealing!
As out of eyes that never wept
　　The blesséd tears come stealing.

You whisper a word for me alone
　　And give me a wreath, dream-begotten . . .
I wake—and the cypress-wreath is gone,
　　And the word is quite forgotten!

63.

Das ist ein Brausen und Heulen

A howling storm is brewing,
　　The wind and rain are wild;
And what can my love be doing,
　　That pale and frightened child?

Lyrical Intermezzo

There at the window dreaming,
  I see her, worn and white;
With eyes no longer beaming,
  She stares into the night.

64.

Der Herbstwind rüttelt die Bäume

Wild Autumn shakes the branches,
  The night is damp and cold;
I ride through a lonely forest,
  Wrapped in my cloak's gray fold.

And, as I ride, my fancies
  Fly faster along the road;
They bear me, light and eager,
  To her beloved abode.

The dogs awake; the torches
  Flare, and the whole house stirs;
I storm the spiral staircase
  And mount, with a clatter of spurs.

Lo, in her own soft chamber,
  Warm with its fragrant charms,
My love awaits me, smiling—
  I fly to her open arms . . .

I hear the oak-tree speaking;
  The wind, in the branches, screams:
"What wouldst thou, oh wild horseman—
  Thou, and thy wilder dreams!"

65.

Es fällt ein Stern herunter

A star, a star is falling
    Out of the glittering sky!
The star of Love! I watch it
    Sink in the depths and die.

The leaves and buds are falling
    From many an apple-tree;
I watch the mirthful breezes
    Embrace them wantonly.

A swan, a swan is singing;
    I watch it floating by;
And, drooping low and lower,
    The song and singer die.

It is so dark and silent!
    The star that burned so long
Is dust; the leaves are ashes;
    Hushed is the swan's last song.

66.

Der Traumgott bracht' mich in ein Riesenschloss

The Dream-God led me to a castle grim
    Full of strange lights, strange scents and stranger glamor;
And through great labyrinths there seemed to swim
    Wild multitudes whom nothing could enamor.
Onward they swept, through halls and portals dim,
    Wringing pale hands with an incessant clamor.
Maidens and knights I saw among the throng
And, with the torrent, I was borne along.

When suddenly I was alone—and lo,
   I could not find a single face whatever.
Through frowning aisles and winding rooms I go;
   Fiercely impelled by one intense endeavor.
But oh, my feet are lead, my footsteps slow . . .
   To find the gate, and leave this place forever!
At last, I gain the portals with a prayer,
Fling wide the door and leap . . . *Oh God, who's there!*

My love! Beside that door I saw her stand,
   Pain on her lips and Sorrow's crown above her.
Backward she turned me with a waving hand,
   Threatening or warning, I could not discover . . .
Yet, from her eyes, sprang, like a sweet command,
   A fire that made me once again her lover.
Tender and strong, her very glances spoke
The flaming speech of Love—and I awoke.

67.

Die Mitternacht war kalt und stumm

'Twas midnight, still and very cold;
Through the dark woods I sang and strolled.
I shook the trees with my doleful ditty—
They only nodded their heads, in pity.

68.

Am Kreuzweg wird begraben

They buried him at the cross-roads,
  Whose own hand wrought his doom;
And over him grow blue flowers
  Called the "Poor-Sinner's Bloom."

I stand at the cross-roads sighing,
  Wrapped in a cloak of gloom,
And watch the moonlight trembling
  On the Poor-Sinner's Bloom.

69.

Wo ich bin, mich rings umdunkelt

Now the night grows deeper, stronger;
  Darkness dense about me lies,
Since the stars died; since no longer,
  Love, I can behold your eyes.

Dimmed, forgotten is the dawning
  Of that great and golden light;
At my feet the pit is yawning.
  Take me—stark, eternal Night!

70.

Nacht lag auf meinen Augen

Night lay upon my eyelids,
  Upon my mouth lay lead;
My heart and brain were barren;
  I lay with all the dead.

Lyrical Intermezzo

How long I lay there, sleeping
    I know not; but I gave
A start and turned, for knocking
    Sounded above my grave.

" Rise up, rise up, oh Heinrich,
    The Dawn eternal breaks,
When all the dead are risen
    And deathless Joy awakes."

I cannot rise, my dearest;
    Your face I cannot find—
I've wept until my sorrows
    And tears have made me blind.

" From your dear eyes, oh Heinrich,
    I'll kiss the night away;
And you shall see the angels,
    And Heaven's bright array."

I cannot rise, my dearest,
    Bleeding I lie, unstirred;
Since, to the heart, you stabbed me
    With one sharp, bitter word.

" Softly I'll lay, oh Heinrich,
    My hand upon your heart,
And it will bleed no longer,
    And I will soothe the smart."

I cannot rise, my dearest,
    My head is bleeding too;
'Tis there I fired the pistol
    The day that I lost you!

"With my own hair, oh Heinrich,
   I'll stop the gaping wound,
Press back the streaming torrent
   And make you strong and sound."

So soft her call, so tender,
   She could not be denied—
I strove to rend my coffin
   And struggle to her side . . .

Then all my wounds burst open;
   I felt the torrent break
From head and burning bosom . . .
   And lo, I was awake!

71.

Die alten bösen Lieder

The songs, so old and bitter,
   The dreams so wild and drear,
Let's bury them together—
   What ho! A coffin here!

I have so much to bury
   It never will be done,
Unless the coffin's larger
   Than Heidelberg's great Tun.

And bring a bier to match it
   Of stoutest oaks and pines;
It must be even longer
   Than the long bridge at Mainz.

And also bring twelve giants
  Of mightier brawn and bone
Than Christopher, the sainted,
  Whose shrine is in Cologne.

And in the great sea sink it
  Beneath the proudest wave;
For such a mighty coffin
  Should have a mighty grave . . .

You know what makes my coffin
  So great, so hard to bear?
It holds my love within it,
  And my too heavy care.

THE HOME-COMING
(1823-1824)

1.

In mein gar zu dunkles Leben

In my life's enshrouded darkness
   Once a vision shed its light;
Now, that phantom radiance vanished,
   I am wrapped again in night.

Children, when oppressed by darkness,
   When their happy hearts are cowed,
To allay their fears and trembling
   Sing a song—and sing too loud.

I, a child half-crazed, am singing,
   Singing in the darkness here . . .
If my song is loud and raucous,
   It, at least, has soothed my fear.

2.

Ich weiss nicht, was soll es bedeuten

I do not know why this confronts me,
   This sadness, this echo of pain;
A curious legend still haunts me,
   Still haunts and obsesses my brain:

The air is cool and it darkles;
   Softly the Rhine flows by.
The mountain peak still sparkles
   In the fading flush of the sky.

And on one peak, half-dreaming
  She sits, enthroned and fair;
Like a goddess, dazzling and gleaming,
  She combs her golden hair.

With a golden comb she is combing
  Her hair as she sings a song—
A song that, heard through the gloaming,
  Is magically sweet and strong.

The boatman has heard; it has bound him
  In the throes of a strange, wild love.
He is blind to the reefs that surround him;
  He sees but the vision above.

And lo, the wild waters are springing—
  The boat and the boatman are gone . . .
And this, with her poignant singing,
  The Loreley has done.

3.

Mein Herz, mein Herz ist traurig

My heart is full of sorrow
  Though May is full of cheer;
I stand beside the linden,
  High on the bastion here.

I watch the blue moat idly;
  Gently it flows along.
A boy in a drifting rowboat
  Angles and whistles a song.

The Home-Coming

Beyond, like a quaint, toy village,
   Tiny and many-hued,
Are houses, gardens and people,
   Oxen and meadow and wood.

To bleach their piles of linen
   The laughing maidens come;
The millwheel spatters diamonds;
   I hear its distant hum.

Upon the old, gray tower
   A sentry-box stands low;
And there a chap in scarlet
   Is pacing to and fro.

He practises with his rifle
   That catches the sunset's red;
He shoulders it and presents it—
   Would that he shot me dead!

4.

Im Walde wandl' ich und weine

I pace the greenwood, bitter
   With tears, and as I go
A thrush begins to twitter,
   "Why are you sorrowing so?"

Ask of your sisters, the swallows;
   They know though none of them tells . . .
They nest in the eaves and hollows
   Where the belovèd dwells.

5.

Die Nacht ist feucht und stürmisch

The night is wet and stormy,
   No stars are in the sky;
The boughs in the forest whisper.
   I wander slowly by.

Far off a candle glimmers
   From the forester's lonely room;
But there the light shall not lure me,
   It is too wrapped in gloom.

The sightless grandmother's sitting
   In the high-backed, leather chair;
She listens, stiff as a statue,
   Uncanny and silent there.

Cursing and pacing in anger,
   The forester's red-headed son
Laughs in a burst of fury
   And throws aside his gun.

The girl weeps at her spinning,
   And moistens the flax with her tears.
While at her feet, the dachshund
   Trembles with unknown fears.

The Home-Coming

6.

Als ich auf der Reise zufällig

By chance I met on my journey
   My dear one's family;
Sister and mother and father;
   Smiling, they greeted me.

How was my health—and spirits?
   They? . . . Oh, the same old tale.
I hadn't changed much, they told me,
   Only a trifle pale.

I asked about aunts and cousins
   With interest (save the mark!)
And other such pleasing people,
   And the dog, with his gentle bark.

How was my married sweetheart
   Whom they had left behind?
And smilingly they told me
   That she would soon be confined.

I coughed congratulations,
   And, stammering wretchedly,
I asked them all to greet her
   A thousand times for me.

Then spoke the little sister:
   " That puppy pet of mine
Grew up so big and horrid,
   We drowned him in the Rhine."

The child resembles her sister,
   Sometimes remarkably so—
Those eyes and that way of laughing
   That brought me so much woe.

7.

Wir sassen am Fischerhause

We sat at the hut of the fisher
   And idly watched the sea,
While in the hush of evening
   The mists rose silently.

The yellow lights in the lighthouse
   Shone like a burnished bell,
And in the hazy distance
   One ship still rose and fell.

We spoke of storm and shipwreck,
   Of sailors and their life,
Pulled between sky and water,
   Fierce joy and lusty strife.

We gossiped of distant places,
   Of North and of South we spoke,
Of wild and curious customs,
   And wild and curious folk.

Of how the Ganges sparkles;
   Of great exotic trees;
Of folk who worship the lotus
   Silently, on their knees.

The Home-Coming

Of Lapland; its slovenly people,
    Flat-headed, broad-featured and small,
That do little else but bake fishes
    And squat by the fire and squall. . . .

The girls all listened breathless;
    Then silence, like a spell . . .
The ship could be seen no longer—
    Swiftly the darkness fell.

8.

Du schönes Fischermädchen

Oh lovely fishermaiden,
    Come, bring your boat to land;
And we will sit together
    And whisper, hand in hand.

Oh rest upon my bosom,
    And fear no harm from me.
You give your body daily,
    Unfearing to the sea. . . .

My heart is like the ocean
    With storm and ebb and flow—
And many a pearly treasure
    Burns in the depths below.

9.

Der Mond ist aufgegangen

The yellow moon has risen,
   It slants upon the sea;
And in my arms' soft prison
   My love leans close to me.

Warm with her gentle clinging,
   I lie on the sands, half awake.
" Oh what do you hear in the swinging
   Of the winds, and why do you shake?"

" That's never the wind that is swinging,
   That murmur that troubles me;
It is the mermaidens singing—
   My sisters drowned in the sea."

10.

Auf den Wolken ruht der Mond

The moon is lying on the clouds,
   A giant orange, strangely beaming;
Stretched upon the harsh gray sea
   Long and broadening stripes are gleaming.

Alone I wander by the shore
   Where the waters break and whiten,
And I hear a watery voice,
   And my pulses leap and tighten.

The Home-Coming

Oh, the night is far too long
   And I cannot bear this quiet—
Come, ye lovely water-sprites,
   Dance and rouse the magic riot.

With my head upon your lap,
   Hold me close and never wake me.
Sing me dead and kiss me dead;
   Heart and soul and body—take me!

II.

Eingehüllt in graue Wolken

Wrapped in clouds, as in a mantle,
   Now the great gods sleep together
And I hear them, bravely snoring,
   And we're having awful weather.

It grows wilder; winds are howling
   And the masts are bent like willows.
Who can curb the lordly tempest,
   Put a bridle on the billows!

I can't stop it, let it come then;
   Storms and terrors without number.
I will wrap my mantle round me,
   And, like any god, I'll slumber.

12.

Der Wind zieht seine Hosen an

The wind pulls up his water-spouts,
  His white and foaming breeches;[1]
He whips the waves; he storms and shouts.
  The whole sea heaves and pitches!

From the black skies, a furious might
  Impels the rain's commotion;
It seems as though the ancient Night
  Had come to drown the ocean.

To the mast a vagrant sea-gull clings
  Where, hoarsely shrilling and crying,
As though in despair, she flaps her wings;
  An evil prophesying!

13.

Der Sturm spielt auf zum Tanze

The storm tunes up for dancing,
  It yells and shrieks away;
Huzzah, how the old ship waltzes!
  The night is wild and gay!

A riot of tossing mountains,
  Thus seems the sea to-night.
Here, yawns a sinking chasm;
  There, looms a wall of white.

---

[1] The original of the first two lines:
  Der Wind zieht seine Hosen an,
  Die weissen Wasserhosen!
There is an untranslatable play upon words here; "*Hosen*" being 'breeches' and "*Wasserhosen*" 'water-spouts.'

The Home-Coming

The sound of prayers and puking
   And oaths from the cabin come;
I cling to the mast with a vengeance—
   And wish that I were home!

14.

Wenn ich an deinem Hause

I pass your little window
   The mornings that are fair,
And I am thrilled, my darling,
   Whene'er I see you there.

Your deep brown eyes disturb me,
   They question and condole,
"Who art thou and what ails thee,
   Oh pale and wandering soul?"

I am a German poet,
   In German lands I shine;
And where great names are mentioned
   They're sure to speak of mine.

As for my sickness, darling,
   It's rather a common sign . . .
And where great griefs are mentioned
   They're sure to speak of mine.

15.

Das Meer erglänzte weit hinaus

The vastness of the ocean shone
   In the sunset's final gleaming.
We sat in the fisher's hut alone;
   We sat there, silent and dreaming.

The mist crept up, the waters hove,
  The gulls kept coming and going;
And from your eyes that welled with love
  The quiet tears were flowing.

I saw them fall upon your hand,
  And then, as quickly sinking
Upon my knees, from that white hand
  I drank the tears, unthinking.

And from that hour my life has turned;
  And sorrow leaves me never.
That wretched woman's tears have burned
  And poisoned me forever.

16.

Da droben auf jenem Berge

High up on yonder mountain
  A castle stands, and three
Fair maidens live within it;
  They love me generously.

Saturday, Yetta kissed me;
  Sunday, Julia was free;
On Monday, Kunigunda
  With love near smothered me.

But Tuesday, my three fair charmers
  Gave an imposing fête;
The neighborhood's lords and ladies
  Came riding in wagons of state.

But me they had skipped or forgotten,
   And that was a poor thing to do.
Those gossips, the old aunts and cousins,
   They noticed, and laughed at it too.

17.

Die Lilje meiner Liebe

My sweetheart has a lily
   That dreams by a brook all day,
It turns from me, and stilly
   Its beauty seems to say:

" Go, faithless man, your rapture
   Has left me cold. . . . Depart!
I saw you bend and capture
   The Rose with your faithless heart."

18.

Am fernen Horizonte

Wrapped in the distant sunset,
   Like phantoms in a mist,
I see the town and its towers,
   All rose and amethyst.

A damp sea-breeze is rising;
   The sea grows rough and dark.
With slow and sad precision
   The boatman rows my bark.

The sun looks up a moment,
  Piercing the clouds above,
And shows me, all too clearly,
  The place I lost my love.

19.

Sei mir gegrüsst, du grosse

Greetings to thee, oh city
  Of power and mystery,
That once, within thy bosom,
  Shielded my love for me.

Tell me, oh gates and towers,
  Where is my loved one, where?
Into your care I gave her;
  You should have kept her there.

I do not blame the towers,
  They could not stir where they stood,
When she, with her trunks and boxes,
  Stole off as fast as she could.

The gates, those fools, *they* let her
  Pass through them—and were still.
Well, fools are always willing
  When foolish women will.[1]

---

[1] The original:
> *Die Thore jedoch die liesen*
> *Mein Liebchen entwischen gar still;*
> *Ein Thor ist immer willig,*
> *Wenn eine Thörin will.*

Heine puns here untranslatably on the word "*Thor*," which is either a "gate" or a "fool"; "*Thörin*" being the feminine.

The Home-Coming

20.

So wandl' ich wieder den alten Weg

To old paths and familiar streets
   My footsteps have reverted;
And lo, there stands the Beloved's house,
   So empty and deserted.

How close and narrow the streets have grown;
   The pavement itself is unstable!
The houses topple and seem to fall . . .
   I'm off as fast as I'm able!

21.

Ich trat in jene Hallen

I stood as in a spell
   Where she swore faith undying;
And where her tears once fell
   Serpents were hissing and lying.

22.

Still ist die Nacht, es ruhen die Gassen

The night is still; the streets are quiet;
   My sweetheart dwelt in this house of yore.
Long since she left the city's riot;
   The house still stands as it stood before.

Here, too, there stands a man who gazes
　　On heaven and wrings his hands in despair.
Lo, when his face the moonlight glazes—
　　It is myself that is standing there!

Oh pale, worn shadow, oh phantom double,
　　Why ape my bitter, love-sick tears,
That drove me here to an endless trouble,
　　Many a night in the vanished years.

23.

Wie kannst du ruhig schlafen

How can you sleep so soundly,
　　Knowing I'm living. See,
When the old rage comes on me,
　　What is a yoke to me!

There is a song that tells how
　　A lover dead and brave
Came to his lass at midnight,
　　And brought her to his grave.

Believe me, child of beauty,
　　Bright as the fiercest star,
I live—and am ten times stronger
　　Than all the dead men are!

The Home-Coming

24.

Die Jungfrau schläft in der Kammer

A maiden lies in her chamber
  Lit by a trembling moon;
Outside there rises and echoes
  A waltz's giddy tune.

" I wonder who breaks my slumber;
  I'll go to the window and see—"
And lo, a skeleton stands there;
  He fiddles and sings with glee:

" A dance you swore to give me,
  And you have broken your vow;
To-night there's a ball in the churchyard;
  Come out and dance with me now!"

The maid, as though moved by magic,
  Obeys, and she leaves the house;
The skeleton, fiddling and singing,
  Goes on with its wild carouse.

It fiddles and leaps and dances
  And rattles its bones to the tune;
Its skull keeps nodding and nodding
  Crazily under the moon.

25.

Ich stand in dunkeln Träumen

I stood bewildered, seeing
  Her picture there—and lo,
That fair, beloved likeness
  Began to live and glow.

About her lips there trembled
  A laughter, strange and dear;
And, through the tears of sorrow,
  Her gleaming eyes shone clear.

Wet were my cheeks; the tear-drops
  Were falling fast and free . . .
And oh, I cannot believe it,
  That you are lost to me!

26.

Ich unglücksel'ger Atlas! eine Welt

I, unfortunate Atlas! A whole world,
A monstrous world of sorrows I must carry.
I bear a weight unbearable; a burden
That breaks the heart within me.

Oh foolish heart, you have what you desired!
You would be happy, infinitely happy,
Or infinitely wretched, foolish heart.
And now—now you are wretched!

27.

Die Jahre kommen und gehen

The years keep coming and going,
   Men will arise and depart;
Only one thing is immortal:
   The love that is in my heart.

Oh once, only once, might I see thee,
   Ere I break these fetters in shards,
And kneel to thee dying, and murmur:
   "Madam, my best regards."

28.

Was will die einsame Thräne

What means this lonely tear-drop,
   Misty with ancient pains?
The tragic days have vanished,
   But still this tear remains.

Once it had shining sisters;
   But, with the old delights
And passing griefs, they left me,
   Lost in the windy nights.

Lost, like the mist, those blue orbs;
   Stars with a smiling dart,
That shot the joys and sorrows
   Laughing into my heart.

Even my love has perished,
  A breath that I have drawn . . .
Oh lone, belated tear-drop,
  'Tis time you too were gone.

29.

Der bleiche, herbstliche Halbmond

The pale, autumnal half-moon
  Breaks through the cloudy skies;
Quietly, by the churchyard
  The lonely parsonage lies.

The mother reads in her Bible;
  The son just stares and stares;
The elder daughter dozes;
  The younger one declares:

" Oh Lord, how stupid the days are,
  Endlessly dull and drear!
Only when there's a funeral
  Is there anything doing here."

" You're wrong," says the mother still reading,
  " They've only buried four;
That is, since they laid your father
  There, by the churchyard door."

" Well," yawns the elder daughter,
  " I'll starve no longer with you.
I'll go to the Count to-morrow;
  He's rich, and he loves me too."

The Home-Coming

The son then bursts out laughing,
  " At the ' Star ' there are hunters three;
They're making gold and gladly
  They'll teach the secret to me."

The mother flings her Bible
  At his head, half-crazed with grief,
" That's what you'll be, God help you,
  A common gutter thief! "

Lo, there's a tap at the window;
  They turn to a beckoning hand—
There, in his moldy cassock,
  They see the dead father stand.

30.

Das ist ein schlechtes Wetter

Well, this is awful weather;
  Storming with rain and snow!
I sit at the window staring
  Into the darkness below.

A little glimmering brightness
  Goes down the uncertain street:
A lantern, and a mother
  With tired and stumbling feet.

I think it's eggs and flour
  That the old lady has bought
To bake a cake for her daughter,
  The lazy good-for-naught.

Yawning at home on the sofa
    She lies in front of the blaze—
The golden hair is falling
    Around her golden face.

31.

Man glaubt, dass ich mich gräme

They think that I am tortured
    Beneath a bitter yoke;
And I have come to believe it
    As well as other folk.

Oh little, great-eyed maiden,
    I've told thee time and again,
That beyond words I love thee,
    That Love gnaws my heart in twain.

But in my own room only
    I've said this thing—for see,
When I am in thy presence
    No word escapes from me.

For there were evil angels
    That sealed my lips somehow;
And through these evil angels
    I am so wretched now.

32.

Deine weissen Liljenfinger

Oh, your slim, white lily-fingers,
Only once more might I kiss them;
And, as to my heart I press them,
Lose myself in quiet weeping.

Your clear, violet-eyes pursue me;
Dance before me, day and night.
And I wonder how to answer,
How to solve those sweet, blue riddles.

33.

"Hat sie sich denn nie geäussert"

" Has she never even shown you
   That your hot avowals moved her?
Did her dark eyes tell you nothing,
   When you swore how much you loved her?

" Could you never find an entrance
   To her soul through sighs and glances? . . .
And they say you're not a donkey,
   But a Hero of Romances!"

34.

Sie liebten sich beide, doch keiner

They loved one another, though neither
    Would speak to the other thereof;
They looked at each other like strangers
    The while they were dying of love.

They parted; and only in visions
    They met, and the dream soon fled.
And at last these two were buried—
    They scarcely knew they were dead.

35.

Und als ich euch meine Schmerzen geklagt

When I told of my sorrows that wounded and tore
    You answered with yawns and nothing more.
But now, since I've added a lyrical phrase
    And put them in verse, you are lavish with praise!

The Home-Coming

And often like old folk we gossiped,
  Aping their serious ways;
Complaining how things were better
  In ' the dead and dear old days.'

How Love and Faith and Honor
  Were lost without regret;
How coffee was so expensive,
  And money so hard to get! . . .

Gone are the plays of childhood,
  And all things seem a wraith—
Time and the world and money,
  And Love and Honor and Faith.

39.

Das Herz ist mir bedrückt, und sehnlich

My heart is crushed with grief, for sadly
  I think of old times, clean of strife,
When all the world went far from badly,
  And people lived a normal life.

But now the world seems madly driven;
  Scrambling to pull and push ahead!
Dead is the good Lord up in Heaven,
  And down below the devil's dead.

All things, with this eternal shoving,
  Become a gray and sodden brawl;
And if it were not for a little loving
  There'd be no rest for us at all.

40.

Wie der Mond sich leuchtend dränget

As the moon through heavy cloud-drifts
   Bursts with his effulgent rays,
So a shining memory rises
   From the old and darkened days.

On the deck we sat, and drifted
   Down the Rhine as on a throne;
And the banks, bright green with summer,
   In the radiant twilight shone.

And there was a gracious lady;
   At her feet I sat and dreamed.
On that pale, dear face the ruddy,
   Burnished gold of sunset gleamed.

Lutes were ringing, boys were singing;
   Happiness on every side!
And the vault of heaven grew bluer,
   And the very soul grew wide.

And there passed, as in a legend,
   Cliff and castle, wood and field . . .
And I saw them through her beauty;
   In her eyes they lay revealed.

41.

Im Traum sah ich die Geliebte

I saw in a dream the Belovéd,
   A woman careworn and gray;
That radiant, blossoming body
   Withered and fallen away.

One child in her arms she carried,
   And one by her hand was led;
And struggle and sorrow were written
   In her look, her clothes, her tread.

She stumbled toward the market,
   And there I met her, and she
Saw me, and I began speaking
   Calmly and mournfully:

"Oh, come with me to my dwelling,
   For thou art sick and pale;
And meat and drink I'll work for
   To make thee whole and hale.

"And I will tend and cherish
   Thy children undefiled;
But thee, before all others,
   Thou poor, unfortunate child.

"And I will never speak of
   My love so torn and deep.
And when at last thou diest,
   Upon thy grave I'll weep."

42.

Teurer Freund! Was soll es nützen

Why, my friend, this same old fretting,
  In the same, monotonous fashion?
Will you be forever setting
  On the addled eggs of passion?

" Ah! It's no small task to tackle!
  First the chicks come, thin and sickly;
Then, when they begin to cackle,
  In a book you clap them, quickly."

43.

Werdet nur nicht ungeduldig

Listen; do not grow impatient,
  Though I keep the old note ringing,
And you hear the old heart-sickness,
  Even in my latest singing.

Only wait—these dying echoes
  Soon will cease; and with new power,
Lo, a new, poetic Springtime
  In a heart that's healed will flower.

The Home-Coming

44.

Nun ist es Zeit, dass ich mit Verstand

Now it is time that I should start
  And leave all folly behind me.
As comic actor I've played my part
  In a comedy that was assigned me.

The settings were painted brilliant and bold
  In the latest romantic fashions;
My knightly mantle was splendid with gold;
  I thrilled with the noblest passions.

And now at last I must say good-by
  To speeches once distracting . . .
But I am wretched and I sigh
  As though I still were acting.

Oh God! unknown I spoke in jest
  The things I felt most deeply;
I've acted, with death in my very breast,
  The dying hero, cheaply.

45.

Den König Wiswamitra

The good king Wiswamitra
  Has little quiet now;
He'll fight, he'll fret, he'll famish
  To get Wasishta's cow.

Oh, good king Wiswamitra,
  Oh, what an ox art thou;
Such fastings, such great torments—
  And all for that one cow!

46.

Herz, mein Herz, sei nicht beklommen

Heart, my heart, let naught o'ercome you;
  Bear your destiny and pain.
  Spring will bring you back again
What the Winter's taken from you.

And how much is left! The small things
  And the whole of earth is fair!
  Heart, you never need despair—
You can love, not one, but all things!

47.

Du bist wie eine Blume

Child, you are like a flower,
  So sweet and pure and fair;
I look at you and sadness
  Comes on me, like a prayer.

I must lay my hands on your forehead
  And pray God to be sure
To keep you forever and always
  So sweet and fair—and pure.

The Home-Coming

48.

Kind! es ware dein Verderben

Child, I know 'twould be your ruin,
   And my thoughts keep guard and turn there;
That your heart may not be kindled
   With the love that used to burn there.

But my too successful triumph
   Somehow does not quite delight me.
And I keep on thinking, hoping
   You might love me yet—despite me.

49.

Wenn ich auf dem Lager liege

When I lie down for comfort
   Upon the pillows of night,
There rises and floats before me
   A phantom clothed in light.

As soon as smiling Slumber
   With soft hands locks my eyes,
Into my dream the vision
   Creeps with a sweet surprise.

But even with the morning
   The dream persists and stays;
The sunlight cannot melt it—
   I carry it all my days.

50.

Mädchen mit dem roten Mündchen

Girl whose mouth is red and laughing;
    Girl whose eyes are soft and bright,
All my being moves about you,
    Thinking of you day and night.

Long, how long, this winter evening;
    And I yearn the whole night through
To be sitting, talking lightly,
    In the little room with you.

To my lips I would be pressing,
    Love, your slender, tender hand;
And my tears would tremble, blessing
    That beloved and blessèd hand.

51.

Mag da draussen Schnee sich türmen

Snows and storms may whirl in torrents;
And I watch, without abhorrence,
Hail at all my windows storming;
For they never seem alarming
While my heart can hold this grace:
Spring,—and one dear, Spring-like face.

52.

Verriet mein blasses Angesicht

Did not my pallid face betray
  The passion that I bore you?
And did you think my haughty lips
  Would, beggar-like, implore you?

These haughty lips were only made
  For kisses, jests and lying—
They'd form a mocking, scornful word
  Even though I were dying.

53.

" Teurer Freund, du bist verliebt"

" Ah, my friend, you are in love
  And new torments chain you tighter;
For your brain is growing duller
  As your foolish heart grows lighter.

" Yes, my friend, you are in love,
  Though the truth is unconfessed;
Why, I see your heart's blood glowing—
  Blushing, even through your vest!"

54.

Ich wollte bei dir weilen

I sought your side, the only
    Peace that I ever knew;
You left me, worn and lonely—
    You had so much to do.

I said I gave you wholly
    Body and soul; and how
You laughed, laughed long and drolly,
    And made a twinkling bow.

With all these things you tried me;
    You even dared do this:
You roused and then denied me
    A single, parting kiss.

Think not because of my snarling
    I'll shoot myself at your door! . . .
All this, my precious darling,
    Has happened to me before.

55.

Saphire sind die Augen dein

Sapphires are those eyes of yours,
    None lovelier or braver;
Thrice happy is the lucky man
    On whom they shine with favor.

The Home-Coming

Your heart is a warm diamond,
   A light that never dwindles.
Thrice happy is the lucky man
   For whom that fire kindles.

Twin rubies are those lips of yours,
   A rich and radiant measure.
Thrice happy is the lucky man
   Who can possess this treasure.

Oh, could I know that lucky man,
   And find that happy lover,
Nicely alone in some deep wood—
   His luck would soon be over.

56.

Habe mich mit Liebesreden

I have lied to win you, precious;
   Now my breast against yours burns.
And I lie in my own meshes,
   And the jest to earnest turns.

And if ever you should leave me,
   With a jest, as is your right,
Earnestly, while fiends receive me,
   I will shoot myself that night.

57.

Zu fragmentarisch ist Welt und Leben

Life in this world is a muddled existence—
Our German professor will give me assistance.
He knows how to whip the whole thing into order;
He'll make a neat System and keep it in line.
With scraps from his nightcap and dressing-gown's border
He'd fill all the gaps in Creation's design.

58.

Ich hab' mir lang den Kopf zerbrochen

My head and brain are almost broken
    With dreams and thinking, night and day;
But now your eyes have solved the problem,
    They sweep my hesitance away.

And I will come to you quite boldly,
    And meet your eyes' sweet, silent call.
And once again I am a lover . . .
    Something I cannot grasp at all.

59.

Sie haben heut Abend Gesellschaft

They're having a party this evening
    And the house is gay with light.
Above, at a brilliant window,
    A shadow trembles in sight.

The Home-Coming

You see me not; in darkness
  I move alone, apart;
How little can you see, then,
  Into my darkened heart.

My darkened heart still loves you,
  Loves you and tortures me,
And breaks and lies here bleeding—
  But you can never see.

60.

Ich wollt' meine Schmerzen ergössen

Oh, that I could capture my sadness
  And pour it all into one word;
The glad-hearted breezes would lift it
  And carry it off, like a bird.

They'd bear it to you, oh belovéd,
  That word of my passionate care;
And every hour you'd hear it,
  'Twould follow you everywhere.

Yes, when you have scarce closed your
    eyelids,
  And slumber over them streams,
That word will arise and pursue you—
  Even into your dreams.

61.

Du hast Diamanten und Perlen

You've pearls and you've diamonds, my dearest,
   You've all that most mortals revere;
And oh, your blue eyes are the fairest—
   What else could you ask for, my dear?

Upon those blue eyes, my dearest,
   I've written for many a year
A host of immortal poems—
   What else could you ask for, my dear?

And with those blue eyes, my dearest,
   You wrought a bright torture here,
And lightly you led me to ruin—
   What else could you ask for, my dear?

62.

Wer zum erstenmale liebt

He who, for the first time, loves,
Even vainly, is a God.
But the man who loves again,
And still vainly, is a fool.

Such a fool am I; the second
Time I love, still unrequited.
Sun and moon and stars are laughing;
And I laugh with them—and perish.

63.

Zu der Lauheit und der Flauheit

In your tepid soul and vapid,
   There's no strength to stand the shocks
Of my wild love, with its rapid
   Force that breaks a path through rocks.

You, you want Love's broad, safe high-roads,
   And a husband's arm through life;
Scorning all the glades and by-roads,—
   Just a prim and pregnant wife.

64.

O, mein gnädiges Fräulein, erlaubt

  Oh loveliest of ladies, may
     This pale son of the Muses,
  Upon thy swan-like bosom lay
     His head with Love's own bruises.

  "Oh sir! To say such things to me
  Out loud—in front of company!"

65.

Gaben mir Rat und gute Lehren

Of words and advice they were the donors;
They even promised me lavish honors.
My future was rosy, my fame would be great;
They'd be my patrons—I only need wait.

But still, with all their patronization,
I would have died of slow starvation,
Except for a man who chanced to be made
Of splendid stuff and who came to my aid.

Excellent fellow! I look on and let him
Work for my dinner; I'll never forget him!
Ah, it's a pity that I never can
Kiss him—for I am that worthy man.

66.

Diesen liebenswürd'gen Jüngling

This most amiable youngster
   Can't be spoken of too highly;
Oft with wine, liqueurs and oysters
   He regales me, almost shyly.

Charming are his coat and trousers
   And 'nis ties are most appealing;
And he comes here every morning
   Just to ask me how I'm feeling.

Of my wide renown he gushes,
   Of my grace, my wit and humor;
And he swears to serve and help me,
   Grieving that he cannot do more.

And at many an evening party
   'Mid the ladies' panegyrics,
With inspired voice and features
   He recites my deathless lyrics.

The Home-Coming

Oh, to find so rare a fellow
   Makes me see the whole world gaily;
In these sorry times, above all,
   When his betters vanish daily.

67.

Mir träumt: ich bin dir liebe Gott

I dreamt I was the dear Lord God
   And sat in Heaven gaily,
The angels thronged about my feet
   And praised my verses daily.

And cakes I ate and sweetmeats too,
   My costly taste displaying.
I washed them down with rare old wines,
   Without a thought of paying.

But the inaction bored me so,
   I longed once more to revel;
I thought, were I not God Himself,
   I'd rather be the devil.

"Ho, long-legged Gabriel," I called,
   "Put on thy boots, I prithee;
Seek out my good old friend Eugene
   And fetch him quickly with thee.

"Seek him not at the college halls,
   Seek him where wine inspires;
Seek him not at St. Hedwig's church—
   Seek him at Ma'm'selle Meyer's."

The angel spread his plumes and flew
　　Swift as a wingéd stallion,
And found and carried up to me
　　My friend, the old rapscallion.

"Yes, lad, I am the Lord Himself,
　　I rule each great and dumb thing;
I always told you some fine day
　　I would amount to something.

"And I work wonders every hour,
　　Things that would quite enthuse you;
To-day, for instance, I will change
　　All Berlin, to amuse you.

"The cobble-stones in every street
　　Shall split; and in their moister,
New-opened centers shall be found,
　　Juicy and fresh—an oyster!

"A rain of gentle lemon-juice
　　Shall fall on them, bestowing
A grace; and lo, through all the streets
　　Rhine wine shall keep on flowing.

"See how the folk of Berlin run;
　　Their joy's too great to utter;
The heads of all the City Courts
　　Are drinking from the gutter.

"And look how glad the poets are,
　　How hungrily they rally!
The ensigns and lieutenants too
　　Lap up each street and alley.

"The soldiers tho' are cleverest,
   Their shrewdness they display there.
They know that miracles like this
   Don't happen every day there."

68.

Von schönen Lippen fortgedrängt, getrieben

Torn from bright lips I loved; departing sadly
   From those warm eyes that held me in their heaven.
I would have stayed another day, and gladly,
   But then the coach came up—and I was driven.

Child, that is life! A constant cry and wailing;
   A constant parting, though your arms enfold me.
Keep me—but see, no heart can be unfailing;
   Even your eyes were powerless to hold me.

69.

Wir fuhren allein im dunkeln

Alone in the dim post-wagon
   We sat and rode through the night;
Closely together we nestled,
   With laughter the hours were light.

But oh, my love, next morning—
  And how we stared to find,
Sitting between us, Cupid;
  The boy that seemed so blind![1]

70.

Wie dunkle Träume stehen

Like a dark dream the houses
  Stretch in a ghastly row;
Wrapped in my mantle softly
  I pass them, silent and slow.

The tower of the cathedral
  Rings with the midnight hour;
And now my sweetheart is waiting
  With all of her charms in flower.

The moon's my friend and companion,
  He lights the ways that are dim;
And as I come to her dwelling
  Gladly I call to him:

---

[1] The original:

*Doch als es Morgens tagte,
  Mein Kind, wie staunten wir!
Denn zwischen uns sass Amor,
  Der blinde Passagier.*

It is possible that in "*der blinde Passagier*" Heine was half-punning on a bit of German slang. A "blind passenger" being one who, like a stowaway, gets in anywhere without paying; one who, in our own street idiom, "beats his way."

The Home-Coming

"I thank you, good old comrade,
  Through you no path was furled;
And now, since I must leave you,
  Go light the rest of the world.

"And if you find a lover
  Heaving a lonely sigh,
Console him as you consoled me,
  My friend, in the days gone by."

71.

Hast du die Lippen mir wund geküsst

With kisses my lips were wounded by you,
  So kiss them well again;
And if by evening you are not through,
  You need not hurry then.

For you have still the whole, long night,
  Darling, to comfort me!
And what long kisses and what delight
  In such a night may be.

72.

Und bist du erst mein ehlich Weib

And when you're once my wedded wife
  You'll be an envied one, dear;
For then you'll live the happiest life
  With nought but pleasure and fun, dear.

And if you should scold I will not curse,
 'Twill be a matter of course, dear;
But ah, should you disdain my verse,
 I'll get me a divorce, dear.

73.

Als sie mich umschlang mit zärtlichem Pressen

When I am enwrapped in her tender embraces
 My soul seeks the skies like a thing that is driven!
I let it ascend; and meanwhile no place is
 As sweet as her lips, where I drink draughts of heaven.

74.

In den Küssen, welche Lüge

Oh what lies there are in kisses!
 And their guile so well prepared!
Sweet the snaring is; but this is
 Sweeter still, to be ensnared.

Though your protests overwhelm me,
 Still I know what you'll allow.
Yet I'll swear by all you tell me;
 I'll believe all you avow.

75.

An deine schneeweisse Schulter

Upon your snow-white shoulder
  My weary head's at rest,
And I can hear the longing
  That stirs within your breast.

The blue Hussars come bugling,
  Come riding past your door;
And to-morrow, my love, you'll leave me
  And I shall see you no more.

But though you will leave me to-morrow,
  To-day you are wholly mine;
To-day you shall bless me doubly,
  Closer your arms shall twine.

76.

Es blasen die blauen Husaren

The blue Hussars go bugling
  Out of the town and away;
I come to you now, my sweetheart,
  Bringing a rose bouquet.

That was a mad, wild uproar;
  Crowding in every part!
But there was a place for many,
  Even in your small heart.

77.

Habe auch in jungen Jahren

In my youth when Love was yearning,
I was often sad, and burning
    Like a cord of wood.
Now the price of fuel's higher,
And the cost has quenched the fire,
    Ma foi! and that is good.

Think of this, my pretty darlings,
Cease your silly tears and quarrelings;
    Stupid griefs and harms.
You have Life, that precious bubble;
So forget Love's ancient trouble,
    Ma foi! within my arms.

78.

Bist du wirklich mir so feindlich

Have you really grown to hate me?
    Is the dreaded change completed?
Then the world shall hear my grievance,
    Hear how badly I've been treated.

Oh, ungrateful lips, how could ye
    Utter such a shameful story
Of the man whose kisses thrilled ye
    In those days of perished glory.

79.

Ach, die Augen sind es wieder

Ah, those eyes again which always
   Made my welcome seem completer;
And those lips again which always
   Made my harsh life somehow sweeter.

And the voice is just as always,
   When its lightest whisper gladdened.
Only *I* am not as always;
   I am home, but changed and saddened.

Now I feel white arms about me
   Close and passionately twining,—
Yet I lie upon her bosom
   Unresponsive and repining.

80.

Himmlisch war's, wenn ich bezwang

'Tis a heavenly pleasure indeed,
   Curbing Passion's wild excess;
And when I do not succeed
   'Tis a pleasure none the less.

81.

Selten habt ihr mich verstanden

Hard to understand your gabble;
   And my thoughts you fail to reach.
Only when in filth we dabble
   Do we find a common speech.

82.

Doch die Kastraten klagten

And still the eunuchs grumbled,
   Whene'er my voice arose;
They grumbled as they mumbled
   My songs were far too gross.

And oh, how sweetly thrilling
   Their little voices were;
Their light and limpid trilling
   Made such a pretty stir.

They sang of Love, the leaping
   Flood that engulfs the heart . . .
The ladies all were weeping
   At such a feast of Art!

83.

Auf den Wällen Salamankas

On the walls of Salamanca
   Where the very winds are fonder,
Slowly, with my lovely Donna,
   In the summer dusk we wander.

And my arm is bent about her
   Slender body, and it lingers
As I feel her haughty bosom
   Heave beneath my happy fingers.

But a vague and threatening whisper
   From the linden makes me gloomy;
And the millwheel's evil murmur
   Sends a dark foreboding through me.

"Ah Señora, something tells me
   Nevermore we two shall wander
On the walls of Salamanca,
   Where the very winds are fonder."

84.

Kaum sahen wir uns, und an Augen und Stimmen

As soon as we met we were 'wrapped in each other,
   Your eyes and your voice showed you would not resist;
And had it not been for that dragon, your mother,
   There, in that instant, I think we'd have kissed.

To-morrow, alas, I must leave the quaint city
   And go the old way, as if bound by a spell.
And you will look down from your window in pity;
   And I—I will wave back a friendly farewell.

85.

Über die Berge steigt schon die Sonne

Over the mountains the sun throws his fire;
   The bells of the lambs in the distance are low.
My love and my lamb, my own sun of desire,
   Once more I would see you before I must go.

I gaze at her window, impatient and muffled—
   " My child, fare thee well; I am parting from thee! "
In vain! Nothing moves, not a curtain is ruffled;
   For still she lies sleeping and dreaming . . . of me?

86.

Zu Halle auf dem Markt

   In Halle's market-place
   There stand two mighty lions.
   Observe their hollow boldness; see
   How quickly men have tamed them!

   In Halle's market-place
   There stands a mighty giant.
   He has a sword, but wields it not.
   Some fear has petrified him.

The Home-Coming

In Halle's market-place
There stands a great cathedral,
Where city-folk and others too
Have plenty of room to pray in.

87.

Schöne, wirtschaftliche Dame

Lovely and efficient lady,
   House and farm are well endowed;
And your cellar's well appointed,
   And your fields are all well ploughed.

In your clean and shining garden
   Weeds can never raise their heads;
And the straw, when threshing's over,
   Will be used to stuff the beds.

But your heart and lips, fair lady,
   Fallow lie, as hard as stone;
And the bed is but half useful
   Where you lie and sleep—alone.

88.

Dämmernd liegt der Sommerabend

Softly now the summer twilight
   Lies upon the woods and meadows;
   And a golden moon looks downward
With a comforting and shy light.

By the brook and in its islands
  Crickets chirp; the water murmurs.
And the wanderer hears a plashing
And a breathing in the silence.

There, alone, unclad, unfrightened,
  See, a water-nymph is bathing.
  How those white limbs in the water
And the moon are doubly whitened!

89.

Nacht liegt auf den fremden Wegen

Night lies on the strange, dark roadways;
  Weary limbs and heart distress me . . .
Ah, sweet moon, through you my load weighs
  Lighter, as your soft beams bless me.

Radiant moon, your gentle wonder
  Sends Night's ancient terrors reeling;
All my fears are torn asunder,
  And the happy tears come healing.

90.

Der Tod, das ist die kühle Nacht

Death—it is but the long, cool night;
  And Life is but a sultry day.
  It darkens, and I slumber;
I am weary of the light.

The Home-Coming

Over my bed a strange tree gleams,
    And there a nightingale is loud;
    She sings of love, love only . . .
I hear it in my dreams.

91.

" Sag, wo ist dein schönes Liebchen"

"Where is now your precious darling,
    That you sang about so sweetly,
When the magic, flaming torrent
    Fired and filled your heart completely?"

Ah, that fire is extinguished,
    And my heart no longer flashes;
And this book's an urn containing
    All my love—and all its ashes.

DUSK OF THE GODS

Der Mai ist da mit seinen goldnen Lichtern

The May is here with all her golden glamor,
And silken zephyrs and warm, spicy odors.
She lures me, laughing, with her snowy blossoms,
And greets me with the thousand eyes of violets.
She spreads a wide green carpet rich with flowers,
Woven throughout with sun and morning dew;
And thus she calls to all her well-loved mortals.
The pale-faced, shut-in people hear her first;
The men put on their fancy trousers
And Sunday coats with gold and glassy buttons;
The women all wear white—for innocence;

Youths start to train and twirl the vernal mustache;
Young girls begin a heaving of the bosom;
The city poets stuff into their pockets
Pencil and pad and opera-glass! and gladly
The gaily-colored crowds make for the gates,
And camp outside upon the verdant hillsides,
Amazed to see the trees so busily growing;
Playing with sweet and brightly-colored flowers,
Hearing the songs of birds, clear-toned and joyful,
And shouting exultations up to heaven.

May called upon me too. She knocked three times
Upon my door and cried, "I am the May!
Thou pallid dreamer, come,—and I will kiss thee!"
I held my door closed tight, and called to her:
Your lures are all in vain, false visitor.
I have seen through you, May; I have seen through
The world's vast plan—and I have looked too long,
And much too deep; for all my joy has vanished,
And deathless troubles rankle in my heart.
I see right through the hard and stony cover
Of all men's houses and of all men's hearts,
And see in both lies and deceit and torture.
I read men's thoughts by looking at their faces,
Most of them evil. In the blush of maidens
I see the trembling wish beneath the shame;
Upon Youth's proud and visionary head
I see the cap-and-bells of stupid folly;
And twisted phantom-pictures, crazy shadows
Are all I see,—until I scarcely know
If earth's a madhouse or a hospital.

Dusk of the Gods

I see right through the earth to its foundations,
As though 'twere crystal, and I see the horrors
That May, with all her green and gladdening cover,
Hides all in vain. I see the dead:
They lie below there in their narrow coffins,
Their still hands folded and their blind eyes open;
White are their robes and whiter still their faces.
And through black lips the yellow worms are crawling.
I see the son sitting beside his mistress,
Taking their pleasure on his father's grave;
The nightingales sing mocking songs around them;
The gentle meadow-flowers grin and chuckle.
Deep in his grave the father stirs and shivers—
And Mother Earth is torn with painful spasms.

Oh Earth, poor Earth, I know your pains and sorrows;
I see the fire raging in your bosom,
I see you bleeding from a thousand veins,
I see your countless wounds torn wide and gaping,
Pouring out streams of flame and smoke and blood.
I see those stark, defiant sons of giants,
Your primal brood, climb from the gloomy chasms
Swinging red torches in their horny hands.
They fix their iron ladders to the skies
And rush to storm the citadel of Heaven.
Black dwarfs swarm hotly after them; and, crackling,
The golden stars crumble to dust and ashes.
Dark, impious hands tear down the golden curtain
From God's own shrine; and with a frightful shrieking
The holy angels fall upon their faces.
Upon his throne a pale and frightened God
Plucks off his diadem and tears his hair . . .
And still the savage horde draws nearer, nearer.

The giants hurl their rain of blazing torches
Into the vaults of heaven; the dwarfs belabor
The backs of angels with their flaming scourges.
In pain the stricken spirits cringe and cower,
And by the hair they are torn down and vanquished.

And there, I see my own dear angel stand
With her blonde locks, her sweet, inspiring features,
And with eternal love about her lips,
And with great blessings in her great, blue eyes—
When lo, a frightful, black and evil goblin
Tears from the ground my pale and trembling angel.
Grinning, he gloats upon her noble beauty,
And clasps her close with tightening embraces . . .

A shriek of horror cleaves the universe,
Its pillars topple, Earth and Heaven crumple . . .
And Night resumes its black and ancient rule.

DONNA CLARA

In dem abendlichen Garten

In the evening-colored garden
Wanders the Alcalde's daughter;
Trumpets' and the drums' rejoicings
Rise and echo from the castle.

"Oh, I weary of the dances,
And the cloying, fatuous phrases
Of the knights, who, bowing deeply,
To the sun itself compare me.

Donna Clara

"Everything seems dull and tiresome
Since by moonlight I beheld him,
Him, my hero, whose sweet lute-strings
Draw me nightly to my window.

"How he stood; so slim and fiery,
And his eyes were burning boldly
From his pale and classic features—
Looking like St. George, the valiant."

Thus mused lovely Donna Clara,
Gazing at the ground beneath her;
As she looked up—lo, the handsome
Unknown knight stood there before her.

Clasping hands with trembling passion,
Now they wander in the moonlight;
Now the flattering breeze is friendly;
Great, enchanted roses greet them.

Great, enchanted roses greet them,
Redder than love's flaming heralds . . .
"Ah, but tell me, my belovèd,
Why these deep and sudden blushes."

"Gnats were stinging me, my dearest,
And I hate these gnats in summer;
Hate them, love, as though they might be
Nasty Jews with long, hooked noses."

"Jews and gnats—let us forget them,"
Says the knight, with soft persuasion . . .
From the almond tree a thousand
Flower-flakes of white are falling.

Flower-flakes of white are falling,
And their perfume spills about them—
"Ah, but tell me, my belovèd,
Is your heart mine, and mine only?"

"Yes, I love but you, my dearest,
And I swear it by the Saviour
Whom the Jews, God's curse upon them,
Did betray and foully murder."

"Jews and Saviour—let's forget them,"
Says the knight, with soft persuasion . . .
Far-off in the dreamy distance
Lilies gleam with light surrounded.

Lilies gleam, with light surrounded,
Gazing at the stars above them.—
"Ah, but tell me, my belovèd,
Have you not perhaps sworn falsely?"

"Nothing's false in me, my dearest;
Just as in my breast there courses
Not a drop of blood that's Moorish,
Nor a taint of Jewish foulness."

"Jews and Moors—let us forget them,"
Says the knight, with soft persuasion,
And, into a grove of myrtle,
Guides the fair Alcalde's daughter.

With Love's soft and supple meshes
He has secretly entrapped her.
Short their words, but long their kisses;
And their hearts are running over.

Donna Clara

Like a melting, poignant bride-song,
Sings the nightingale, uplifted;
Like a thousand torchlight dancers
Leap the fireflies from the bushes.

In the grove the stillness deepens.
Nought is heard except the murmurs
Of the wise and nodding myrtle
And the breathing of the flowers.

But the shock of drums and trumpets
Breaks out wildly from the castle,
And it wakes the lovely Clara
From the arms of her belovèd.

"Hark! they call to me, my dearest;
But before we part, pray tell me
What, my love, your own dear name is
That you've hidden so long from me."

And the knight, with gentle laughter,
Presses kisses on her fingers,
On her lips and on her forehead;
And at last he turns and answers:

"I, Señora, your belovèd,
Am the son of the respected,
Erudite and noble Rabbi
Israel of Saragossa."

THE PILGRIMAGE TO KEVLAAR

I.

Am Fenster stand die Mutter

The mother stands by the window,
    The son on the bed doth lie.
"Will you not rise up, William,
    And see the throngs go by?"

"I am so sick, my mother,
    I cannot hear or see;
The thought of my dead Gretchen
    Is all that lives in me."

"Rise up, and then to Kevlaar
    With book and cross we'll go;
God's Mother, She will heal you
    And rid your heart of woe."

The churchly banners flutter,
    Louder the chanting grows;
From Cöln, beside Rhine River,
    The long procession goes.

The mother joins the pilgrims,
    She leads her son in the line,
And they too swell the chorus:
    "Queen Mary, praise be Thine!"

The Pilgrimage to Kevlaar

2.

Die Mutter-Gottes zu Kevlaar

The Mother of God in Kevlaar
  Puts on her finest cloak—
To-day they will keep her busy,
  The crowds of wretched folk.

For all the sick in Kevlaar
  Bring her, as offerings meet,
Limbs made of cunning waxwork,
  Wax arms and waxen feet.

And whoso brings a wax arm
  His arm is healed of its wound,
And whoso brings a wax foot
  His foot grows strong and sound.

Oh many have come to Kevlaar
  On crutches who danced away;
And many whose fingers were palsied
  Can take up the fiddle and play.

The mother took up a wax light
  And moulded therefrom a heart;
"Take this to Mother Mary
  And She will ease the smart."

And sighing he took the wax heart,
  And sighing he knelt and prayed;
The tears in his eyes were trembling,
  And tremblingly he said:

"Oh Holiest of the Holy,
  Virgin, divinely fair,
Empress of all the Heavens
  To Thee I bring my care.

"At Cöln with my aging mother
  I live within the town,
The city of a hundred churches
  And chapels of renown.

"And near us lived my Gretchen
  Who now lies underground—
Mary, I bring Thee a wax heart,
  Heal Thou my heart's great wound.

"Cure Thou my long heart-sickness,
  And daily, rain or shine,
Fervently I will worship.
  Queen Mary, praise be Thine!"

3.

Der kranke Sohn und die Mutter

The heartsick son and the mother
  Were sleeping in the gloom,
And the Mother of God came softly
  And entered the little room.

She bent down over the lover
  And one white hand was drawn
Over his heart so gently . . .
  And, smiling, She was gone.

The Pilgrimage to Kevlaar

In a dream the mother saw this,
  And would have seen still more
But the dogs' loud baying awoke her;
  She stumbled to the floor.

And there, stretched out and quiet,
  He lay—and he was dead.
And on his cheeks the daybreak
  Shone with a sudden red.

She folded her hands and sat there,
  She did not rail or whine;
She murmured over and over,
  "Queen Mary, praise be Thine!"

FROM "THE HARZ JOURNEY"
(1824)

PROLOG

Schwarze Röcke, seidne Strümpfe

Black dress-coats and silken stockings,
  Cuffs of snowy white—beshrew them!
Soft embraces, oily speeches.
  Ah, if but a heart beat through them!

If a storm could stir your shirt-fronts,
  Ruffle them in any fashion!—
Oh, you kill me with your maudlin
  Bursts of imitation passion.

I will go and climb the mountains
  Where the simple huts are standing,
Where the winds blow fresh and freely,
  And a chest may try expanding.

I will go and climb the mountains
  Where the mighty pine-trees tower,
Where the birds and brooks are singing,
  And the heavens grow in power.

Fare ye well, ye polished Salôns,
  Polished folk and polished chaffing—
I will climb the rugged mountains
  And look down upon you, laughing.

A MOUNTAIN IDYL

I.

'Auf dem Berge steht die Hütte

On the mountain stands a cabin
  Wherein lives a mountaineer;
All the evergreens are rustling
  And the moon turns golden here.

In the cabin there's an armchair
  Curiously carved and high.
He who sits in it is lucky;
  And that lucky man am I.

On the footstool there's a maiden,
  In my lap her arms repose;
Eyes like two blue stars that sparkle,
  And her mouth's a crimson rose.

And those dear blue eyes grow larger
  While the wonder in them grows;
And she lays a lily finger
  Shyly on the crimson rose.

No, the mother does not see us,
  For she spins and spins away;
And the father plays the zither,
  Singing some forgotten lay.

From "The Harz Journey"   159

And the maiden whispers softly,
  Softly, almost breathlessly;
While a host of weighty secrets
  Gravely she confides to me.

"But since Auntie died," she tells me,
  "We can never hope to go
To the picnic-grounds at Goslar;
  That's the loveliest place I know.

"On the mountains here, it's lonely;
  Colder far than down below;
And in Winter we are almost
  Lost and buried in the snow.

"Though I'm quite a girl, I tremble
  Like a child that's seized with fright,
At the evil mountain spirits
  And the things they do by night."

Suddenly she stops, as though her
  Own words chill and terrorize;
And she raises both hands quickly,
  Quickly covering her eyes.

In the trees the rustling's louder,
  Faster still the wheel is stirred,
And above the tinkling zither
  Something of the song is heard:

"*Do not fear, my child, my darling,
  Fear no spirit's evil might!
Overhead, my child, my darling,
  Angels guard thee day and night!*"

2.

Tannenbaum, mit grünen Fingern

Now the fir-tree's long, green fingers
   Tap against the window-pane,
And the moon, that quiet listener,
   Sheds a flood of golden rain.

Father, mother, sleeping soundly,
   Snore for hours without a break;
But we two, with lively chatter,
   Keep each other wide awake.

"That you spend much time in praying
   I've my doubts; for always there
Is a sneer about your features
   That was never caused by prayer.

"Oh that sneer, so cold and evil,
   Frightens me and terrifies—
But my terror seems to vanish
   When I see your gentle eyes.

"And I doubt that you believe in
   The inspired Faith of most.
Don't you worship God the Father,
   And the Son and Holy Ghost?" . . .

"Ah, my child, while still an infant,
   While at mother's knee I stood,
I believed in God the Father,
   He whose rule is great and good.

From "The Harz Journey" 161

"He who made the earth we dwell on,
  And the people here below;
He who made sun, moon and planets,
  Teaching them the way to go.

"Then, my child, as I grew older,
  My belief had but begun,
And I mastered many new things,
  And I worshiped God—and Son;

"The Belovèd Son, who, loving,
  Gave us love to bless and guide;
And for his reward, as usual,
  He was scorned and crucified.

"Now that I've matured and learned much,
  Read and roamed from coast to coast,
Now my heart, with deep conviction,
  Bows before the Holy Ghost.

"He has worked the greatest wonders,
  And he works them still; he broke,
Once for all, the tyrant's power,
  And he burst the bondman's yoke.

"All the ancient scars have vanished,
  Justice takes its rightful place;
Now all men are free and equal
  In a pure and noble race.

"Mists and every evil fancy
  That had filled each night and day,
Cares that crowded out our gladness—
  These have all been swept away!

"And a thousand armored champions
  He has sanctified and sent
To fulfill his sacred mission,
  Fired with their high intent.

"Lo, their splendid swords are shining
  And their tossing flags are bright!—
What, my child, you long to look on
  Such a proud and holy knight?

"Well, my child, come here and kiss me;
  Look at me and you can boast
You have known just such a doughty
  Champion of the Holy Ghost."

3.

Still versteckt der Mond sich draussen

Still the bashful moon is hiding
  Close behind the evergreen;
And the lamp upon the table
  Flickers and is scarcely seen.

But those two blue stars are shining
  O'er the heaven of her cheeks;
And the crimson rose is glowing,
  And the lovely child still speaks.

"Tiny goblins, imp-like faeries
  Clean our little cupboard bare;
It is full of food at evening
  And at daylight—nothing's there!

From "The Harz Journey"

"And the thieving Little People
  Skim our cream, our very best;
Then they leave the pans uncovered
  And the cat licks up the rest.

"And that cat's a witch, I know it;
  For she slinks off every night
To the old and ruined castle
  On the haunted mountain-height.

"Once a mighty castle stood there
  Full of armor and romance;
Shining knights and lovely ladies
  Laughed in many a torchlight dance.

"Then an old enchantress cursed it,
  Cursed each stone and winding stair.
Now there's nothing left but ruins;
  And the owls have nested there.

"But my dear old aunt once told me
  If one speaks the Word of Might
At the proper, magic moment,
  And the hour and place be right,

"Then the castle shall be lifted
  From the ruined stones—and then
All the vanished knights and ladies
  Will arise and dance again.

"And who speaks that word of magic,
  Knights and ladies, wall and tower,
All are his; while drums and trumpets
  Hail his new and happy power." . .

Thus the faery legends blossom
  From her mouth, that rose-in-bloom,
While her eyes are pouring starlight
  In the still and darkened room.

Round my hands she winds her golden
  Tresses, binding me at will;
Gives my fingers pretty nicknames;
  Kisses, laughs—and then grows still.

And the hushed room edges closer,
  Watching with a friendly light . . .
Table, chest—it seems I must have
  Seen them all before to-night.

Amiably the old clock gossips,
  And the zither, scarcely heard,
Plays itself with airy fingers;
  And, as in a dream, I'm stirred . . .

This must be the proper hour;
  Yes, the time and place are right.
And I think I feel it gliding
  From my lips—that Word of Might!

Do you see, my child, how quickly
  Midnight trembles now and breaks!
Brooks and pine-trees murmur louder,
  And the ancient mountain wakes.

Clang of zither, elfin voices
  Rise from glens and faery bowers;
And a wild, fantastic Springtime
  Brings a forest full of flowers.

From "The Harz Journey"

Flowers, trembling and audacious,
　Flowers, strangely broad and tall,
Fling their eager scents and colors
　As though passion swayed them all.

Roses, red as flame, and burning
　From the brilliant tumult, rise;
Lilies, like great crystal columns,
　Tower straight into the skies.

And the stars, with fiery longing,
　Great as suns, look down and blaze,
Till the lilies' hearts are flooded
　With those eager, showering rays.

But ourselves, my child, are altered
　More than all of these—and see!
Gleaming torches, silks and jewels
　Shimmer 'round us radiantly.

You, you have become a princess,
　And this hut's a castle tall;
Knights and ladies dance rejoicing;
　And there's magic over all.

Ah, but *I* have won the castle,
　Knights and ladies, wall and tower;
Even you—and drums and trumpets
　Hail my new and happy power!

THE HERD-BOY

König ist der Hirtenknabe

He's a king, this happy herd-boy,
  And his throne's the grassy down;
And the sun above his forehead
  Is his great and golden crown.

At his feet the sheep are lying,
  Flattering courtiers, soft and sly;
And his cavaliers are cattle,
  Stamping arrogantly by.

And the kids are his court-players;
  Flutes of birds that hold carouse
Make a splendid chamber-music
  With the gentle bells of cows.

And they ring and sing so sweetly,
  And the soothing murmurs creep
From the waterfall and forest,
  That the young king falls asleep.

Like a minister, his watch-dog,
  Governs with an open ear—
And his loud, suspicious barking
  Makes the very echoes fear.

Sleepily the young king mutters:
  "Ah, to rule is hard and mean;
How I wish that I were home now
  With my cozy little queen!

"On her dear and queenly bosom
  Soft my regal head would lie;
And I'd find my ancient kingdom
  Shining in each love-lit eye."

ON THE BROCKEN

Heller wird es schon im Osten

Comes a spark, the sun's first glimmer;
  And the eastern sky's in motion.
Far and faint the mountain summits
  Float upon a misty ocean.

Had I seven-league boots, I'd hasten
  With the wind, as fast as telling;
Running on the tops of mountains
  Till I reach my dear one's dwelling.

I would draw the curtains softly
  From her bed, where she lies dreaming;
Softly I would kiss her forehead
  And her lips twin rubies gleaming.

And still softer I would whisper
  In her frail and lily ear, "Love,
Dream we've never lost each other;
  Dream we're lovers still, my dear love."

THE ILSE*

Ich bin die Prinzessin Ilse

I am the Princess Ilse
  And I dwell at Ilsenstein.
Come with me to my castle,
  Thou shalt be blest—and mine.

There I shall bathe thy forehead
  With waters clear and glad,
Until thy pain shall vanish,
  Thou sick and sorrowing lad.

With my white arms about thee
  Upon my breast thou'lt be;
And thou shalt lie there dreaming
  Of faery legendry.

* Here Heine has personified the famous stream and given to it one of those *loreleys* that fill German tradition and verse. As an introduction to this poem he has written, in one of the most beautiful passages of "*Die Harzreise,*" an exquisite description of the river itself, part of which runs:
"It is indescribable, the merriment, the grace and the *naïveté* with which the Ilse leaps down upon and glides over the fantastically piled rocks that she finds in her path . . . like a sprightly girl. Yes, the saying is true, the Ilse is a Princess, who, laughing and blossoming, runs down the mountains. How her white garment of foam glitters in the sunlight! How the silver band about her bosom flutters in the wind! How the diamonds sparkle and flash! The high beech-tree stands near her, like a grave father, secretly smiling at his forward and favorite child; the white birches move about like delighted aunts, who are nevertheless a bit anxious over such daring leaps; and the proud oak looks on like a troubled uncle, who might have to pay for this lovely weather. . . . The flowers on the bank murmur softly 'O, take us along, take us along, dear sister.' But the wild girl, not to be held by anything, runs on . . . and suddenly she seizes the dreaming poet; and over me there streams a flower-like rain of resounding gleams and gleaming sounds, and all my senses lose themselves in a rush of Beauty—and I hear only a sweet and fluty voice singing: '*I am the Princess Ilse,*'" etc.

From "The Harz Journey"

And I shall kiss and hold thee
  As I would kiss and hold
My lover, dear King Heinrich,
  Who now lies dead and cold.

The dead stay dead forever,
  Only the living live;
My laughing heart is leaping,
  I've youth and joy to give.

Then come down to my castle,
  Come to my crystal halls;
The knights and maidens are dancing,
  Happy are all my thralls.

There's rustling of silk and clatter
  Of spurs, and the bright air hums.
The nimble dwarfs are playing
  On fiddles and horns and drums.

But always my arms shall enfold thee
  And I shall keep thee enthralled;
As I stopped the ears of King Heinrich
  When the brazen trumpets called.

THE NORTH SEA
(1825-1826)

FIRST CYCLE

CORONATION

Ihr Lieder! Ihr meine guten Lieder!

Ye songs! Ye valiant songs of mine
Up, up, and arm yourselves!
Let all the trumpets echo,
And lift this blossoming girl
Upon my shield.
For now my restless heart
Longs for her rule, claims her its queen.

Hail to thee, hail—oh youthful Queen!

From the fierce sun at noon
I'll tear the red and gleaming gold,
And it shall be a diadem
For thy belovèd head.
From the great, waving, blue silk tent of
    heaven,
Where all the diamonds of the night are
    flashing,
I'll cut a mighty piece;
And hang it, like a royal mantle,
About thy royal shoulders.
I'll give thee a kingly dower
Of starched and polished sonnets,
Haughty tercets, proud and courtly stanzas.
For Pages I shall give thee my wit;

For Court-fool, my wild imagination;
For Herald, with laughing tears in his
    escutcheon,
My Humors shall serve thee . . .
But I myself, dear Queen,
I humbly kneel before thee,
And present to thee, from the velvet cushion,
With deepest homage,
The little reason
That mercifully has been left me
By thy predecessor in the realm.

TWILIGHT

Am blassen Meeresstrande

On the pale strip of seashore
I sat alone, lost among fugitive thoughts.
The sun was sinking lower and threw
Glowing, red beams upon the water.
And the white, widening line of waves,
Pulled by the urging tide,
Rolled in and rumbled nearer and nearer—
A curious mingling of wailing and whistling,
Of laughing and murmuring, sighing and
    shouting;
And, under it all, the strange croon of the
    ocean.
It was as though I heard forgotten stories,
Ancient and lovely legends,
That once I had heard as a child
From our neighbor's children,
When we, in the summer evening,

On the stone-steps before the door,
Huddled together and listened
With eager hearts,
And sharp, inquisitive eyes . . .
While the growing girls
Sat at the opposite windows;
Their heads showing above the fragrant
    flower-pots,
Faces like roses;
Laughing and moon-illumined.

NIGHT ON THE STRAND

Sternlos und kalt ist die Nacht

The night is starless and cold,
The ocean yawns.
And, flat on his belly, the monstrous North-wind
Sprawls upon the sea.
Wheezing and groaning,
He babbles his hoarse confidences,
Like a crotchety grumbler who has grown good-
    humored;
Babbles to the listening waters.
Wild tales he tells them,
Tales of giants, tales of furious slaughter,
And old-world stories out of Norway.
And, between times, he laughs and bellows out
Incantations from the Eddas,
And oaths and runes
So potent and so darkly magical
That the white sea-children
Leap up turbulently,
In waves of exultation.

Meanwhile, on the flat shore,
Over the surf-dampened sands,
A stranger walks
With a heart that is wilder than winds or waters.
Wherever he tramps
Sparks fly and sea-shells crunch and crumble.
He wraps himself in his gray, gloomy mantle
And strides on quickly through the windy night—
Led safely by the little taper
That beckons and shimmers with promise
From the lonely fisherman's cottage.

Father and brother are out at sea,
And alone,
All alone in the cottage, she sits,
The fisher's lovely daughter.
She sits at the hearth
And listens to the kettle
Singing its droning, drowsy song.
And she shakes fuel and heaps sticks on the fire
And blows on it,
So that the flickering red light
Lights up, with a lovely magic,
That blossoming face,
Those soft white shoulders
That stand out strangely from the coarse, gray shirt;
Shines on those small and careful hands
That are binding the little petticoat
Tighter about her waist.

The North Sea

Suddenly the door springs open
And the nocturnal stranger enters.
Confident with love, his eyes are fixed
On that white, slender girl,
Who trembles before him,
Like a frail and frightened lily.
And he drops his mantle on the ground
And smiles and says:

" Behold, my child, I keep my word;
I come—and with me come
The ancient times, when all the gods
Came down from heaven to the daughters of men,
And embraced them
And begat with them
Sceptre-bearing races of kings,
And heroes, shakers of the world . . .
But, child, do not stand astonished any longer,
Amazed at my divinity;
But get me, I beg of you, some tea with rum,
For it's cold outside.
And on such raw nights
We shiver,—even we, who are immortal;
And, being gods, we catch ungodly sneezings,
With colds and coughing that are almost deathless."

POSEIDON

Die Sonnenlichter spielten

The sun's gay lights were playing
Over the wide and rolling sea.
Far off, and anchored, I saw the ship
That was to take me home;
But the right wind was lacking
And I was still sitting on a white sand-dune
Upon the beach.
And I read the song of Odysseus,
That old and ever-youthful song
From whose leaves, with the breath of the
    ocean rushing through them,
Rises joyfully,
The breath of the gods,
And the radiant Springtime of man,
And the blue, smiling heaven of Hellas.

My noble heart was loyal, and accompanied
The son of Laertes through terror and travail;
Sat down with him, suffered and wept with him
At friendly hearths
Where queens regaled him, spinning purple
    cloths.
It helped him with his lies, and aided his escape
From giants' caverns and the arms of sirens.
It followed him down the Cimmerian night,
Through storm and shipwreck—
It stood with him through struggles past all
    telling.

The North Sea

And then I sighed, "Oh harsh Poseidon,
Thy anger is fearful;
And I myself am afraid
Of my own home-coming."

Scarcely had I spoken,
When the sea was churned into foam
And out of the whitening waters rose
The head of the sea-god,
Sea-weed crowned,
And scornfully he called:

"Have no fear, little poet!
I haven't the least intention to harm
Your poor little boat,
Nor frighten your precious little soul
With a lusty, long-to-be-remembered rocking.
For you, bardlet, have never vexed me.
You have never, that I know of, shaken the smallest turret
Of Priam's holy city.
Nor have you singed a single hair
From the eyelash of my son, Polyphemus;
And, surely, never have you been befriended or counseled
By Pallas Athene, the goddess of Wisdom!"

Thus cried Poseidon
And dived back in the sea.
And at the coarse old sailor's joke
I heard Amphitrite, the fat old fish-wife,
And the stupid daughters of Nereus,
Laughing under the waters.

DECLARATION
Herangedämmert kam der Abend

The evening came, dusk-enshrouded,
The tide tossed in wildly;
And I sat on the beach, watching
The white dance of the breakers.
My bosom heaved like the sea,
And yearning seized me—a keen home-sickness
For you, and your fair image
That rises over all things,
And calls me forever,
Over all and forever,
In the howling of the winds, in the roaring of the sea
And in the sighing clamor of my own heart.

With a light reed I wrote upon the sand
" Agnes, I love you! "
But heartless waves crept up and poured themselves
Over that sweet confession,
And blotted it out.

Frail reed, shifting and treacherous sand,
Unstable waters, I'll trust you no more!
The heaven grows darker, my heart grows wilder;
And with strong hands, from Norway's mighty forests
I'll tear the highest pine;
And dip it deep
In Ætna's glowing crater.
And with such a pen,
Fiery and gigantic,
I'll write upon the darkening dome of heaven
" Agnes, I love you! "

The North Sea

Thus every night that flaming line shall burn
And blaze down from the furthest skies;
And all the vast generations of men
Shall read and thrill with the rapturous words:
" Agnes, I love you!"

From

A NIGHT IN THE CABIN

Das Meer hat seine Perlen

The sea has its pearls,
The heaven its stars,—
But my heart, my heart,
My heart has its love.

The sea and the heaven are great,
But my heart is greater still;
And fairer than pearls or stars
Glistens and sparkles my love.

Oh young and lovely maiden
Come to my fathomless heart;
My soul and the sea and the heavens
Are wasting away with love.

STORM

Es wütet der Sturm

The storm rages now
And whips the waves,
And the waters, boiling and furious,
Tower into a moving waste
Of white and flowing mountains.
And the ship climbs them
Sharply, painfully;
And suddenly plunges down,
Into a black and yawning chasm of flood.

O Sea!
Mother of Venus, born of your quickening
   foam,
Grandmother of Love! Help me!
Already, light of wing, and smelling for
   corpses,
The white and ghostly sea-mew hovers
And whets its bill on the mast-head,
And lusts to feed on my heart
Which rings with the praise of thy daughter;
The heart that thy grandson, the little scamp,
Has taken for plaything.

Fruitless my prayers and entreaties!
My cry dies in the rushing storm,
In the alarum of the wind.
It roars and rattles and whistles and wails—
A madhouse of sounds!
And between times I can hear,
Far off but distinctly,
Magical harp-tones,
Passionate singing,
Soul-melting and soul-tearing—
And I know the voice . . .

Far on the rocky coast of Scotland
Where an old, gray castle
Juts into the boiling sea;
There, at a high-arched window,
A woman stands, lovely and sick at heart,
Delicate-featured and marble-pale.
And she plays on the harp and sings;
And the storm tosses her long hair,
And carries her dark song
Over the wide and darkening sea.

CALM AT SEA

Meeresstille! Ihre Strahlen

Calm at sea! The sun is throwing
Great long beams upon the water,
And the ship ploughs through the furrows,
Through a sea of tossing jewels.

And the bosun on his belly
Softly snores beside the tiller;
While a shrinking, tar-smeared ship's boy
Patches sail beside the foremast.

Underneath the dirt, his cheeks are
Reddening slowly; fear or sorrow
Makes his broad mouth twitch and tremble
And his large, deep eyes are troubled.

For the Captain stands before him,
Storms and swears and scolds him: " Rascal!
Rascal! You've been at the barrel.
Rascal! You have stolen a herring!"

Calm at sea! . . . Above the rollers
Lo, a little fish leaps gaily;
Warms his little head with sunlight,
Flaps his little tail with ardor.

But a sea-gull, from high spaces,
Shoots down on the giddy spratling;
And, her prey held in her talons,
Back into the blue she circles.

PEACE

Hoch am Himmel stand die Sonne

The sun stood high in the heavens
Swathed in white clouds;
The sea was still.
I lay in the helm of the vessel,
Dreamily musing . . . When, half awake
And half asleep, I saw the Christ,
The Saviour of the world.
In a white, waving garment
He walked, tall as a giant,
Over land and sea.
His head rose into the heavens,
His hands were stretched in blessing
Over land and sea;
And, like a heart in his breast,
He carried the sun,
The great, red, burning sun.
And that flaming heart, that fiery splendor,
Poured all its hallowed sunbeams,
And all its tender, compassionate light,
Wide-spread and warming,
Over land and sea.

Clear and happy bells were ringing,
Drawing on the gliding vessel;
Drew, like swans with ropes of roses,
Lightly to a fair, green harbor
Where men lived in a lofty, towering
Sky-scraping city.

The North Sea

Wonder of peace! How quiet the town!
The cries and the clamor were hushed;
The clatter of trade was over.
And, through the clean-swept, echoing streets,
Men in white raiment wandered
Carrying palm-branches.
And where two met in that city,
They gazed at each other with understanding,
And, thrilling with love and a sweet abnegation,
Kissed each other on the brow.
And both looked up
At the glowing heart of the Saviour
That joyfully sacrificed its red blood
In streams of ruddy light.
And they, thrice-blest, would cry,
" Praise be to Jesus Christ! "

If such a conception would have been granted you,
What would you have given,
Dearly belovèd brother!
You who are so weak in the head and the loins
And so strong in the faith!
You who worship the Trinity so religiously
And kiss the cross and the pup and the paw
Of your noble protectress daily.
You who talked yourself into the council
And a place on the bench
And, at last, to a part in the governing
Of that virtuous city,
Where dust and Faith arise,
And the long-suffering Spree, with its holy waters,
Washes the souls and dilutes the tea of the faith-
    ful—
Had you but conceived this vision,

Dearly belovèd,
You would have taken it to market
And offered it in high places.
Your white, simpering features
Would melt with devotion;
And the high and mighty lady,
Enraptured and trembling with bliss,
Would sink, praying, on her knees beside you.
And her eyes, beaming with happiness,
Would promise you an increase of salary
Of a hundred sterling Prussian dollars.
And you would fold your hands and stammer,
" Praise be to Jesus Christ!"

SECOND CYCLE

SEA GREETING

Thalatta! Thalatta!

Thalatta! Thalatta!
Hail to thee, oh Sea, ageless and eternal!
Hail to thee, from a jubilant heart—
Ten thousand times hail!
Hail, as you were hailed by
Ten thousand Grecian hearts;
Calamity-conquering, homeward-hungering,
Immortal Grecian hearts.

The billows rolled higher,
Heaving and howling;
The sun poured eagerly downward
A rain of rosy lights;
The startled sea-gulls
Flew off with loud cries;
And there were sounds of horses stamping,
And the clashing of shields,
And echoes ringing, like a battle-shout:
"Thalatta! Thalatta!"

Hail to thee, Sea, ageless and eternal!
The whisper of your waters is as the speech
    of my own land;
The shimmer and surge of your billowy wastes
Is as the dreams of my childhood;

And old memory reveals in new colors
All of those lovely, wonderful playthings,
All of those glittering Christmas presents,
All of those rosy branches of coral,
Goldfish and pearls and shining sea-shells,—
All that you cherish and guard
Down in your clear and crystal depths.

Oh, how I have suffered in strange places!
My heart lay in my breast
Like a fading flower
In the tin box of a botanist.
It seems as though I had sat through the whole
    Winter,
A sick man in a dismal room,—
And now I leave it!
And suddenly there streams upon me
The emerald Spring, the sun-awakened;
And white branches rustle
And the young flowers look at me
With bright and odorous eyes,
And there's perfume and humming and
    laughter in all that breathes,
And in the blue heavens the very birds are
    singing:
"Thalatta! Thalatta!"

Oh dauntless, home-returning heart,
How often, oh how often,
The barbarian girls of the North have
    assailed you!
How often have they shot burning arrows
With their great, conquering eyes;
How often have they threatened to cleave the
    breast

With curved, two-edged words, sharper than
    swords;
How often their chiseled, hieroglyphic letters
Have beaten on my poor, bewildered brain.
I raised my shield against them vainly.
The arrows whistled, the blows came crashing,
And the barbarian girls of the North
Drove me to the sea—
And now, with a great breath, I greet it,
The long-loved, rescuing sea,
"*Thalatta! Thalatta!*"

SUNSET

Die schöne Sonne

The splendid sun
Has slipped quietly into the sea;
The waving waters are already clouded
With the shadows of night;
Only the afterglow
Stretches a web of gold and rosy lights over
    them.
The restless tide
Urges the billows toward the shore,
And the white waves leap and gambol
Like a flock of woolly lambkins
At evening, when a singing herd-boy
Drives them home.

"How splendid is the Sun!"
Thus, after a long silence, spoke my friend
Who had been walking with me on the beach.
And, half in fun and half in earnest,
He assured me that the sun was a lovely woman
Who had married the old sea-god for convenience.
All day long she wanders happily
Through the high heavens, robed in red and purple,
Blazing with diamonds;
Beloved and worshiped
By every creature in the world;
And all creation is made happy
With the light and warmth of her glance.
But at evening she is forced ruthlessly
To turn back again
To the damp house and the sterile embraces
Of her senile spouse.

"Believe me," my friend continued,
And laughed and sighed and laughed again,
"They live in a sweet wedlock there below!
Either they sleep or else they quarrel
Till the sea above them towers and storms,
And the sailor hears, in the roar of the billows,
How the old one scolds at his wife:
'Whore of the heavens!
Radiant harlot!
All day long you glow for others,
And at night, for me, you are tired and frosty!'

Truly, the girdle of love scarce adorns you,
Yet I am still strangely awed by your beauty;
And if you would give yourself and bless me
Like other great heroes, I'd perish of fear—
A corpse-like goddess you seem to me,
Venus Libitina!
No longer the terrible Ares
Looks at you with the eyes of love.
And how the youthful Phœbus Apollo
Is saddened! His lyre is mute
That joyfully sweetened the feasts of the gods.
Hephæstus is even sadder,
And truly the limping one never again
Shall take Hebe's place
Or busily serve the great assembly
With heavenly nectar.—Time has extinguished
The inextinguishable laughter of the gods.

Ye gods of Greece I have never loved you!
For hateful to me are all the Greeks,
And even the Romans are odious.
Yet holy compassion and tremulous pity
Flow through my heart
When I see you there above me,
Forgotten divinities,
Dead and night-wandering shadows;
Weak as the mist, torn by the wind.—
And when I think how vapid and spineless
The new gods are who have conquered you,
These new, sad gods, who now are the rulers,
Who take joy at our pain in their sheep's cloak
    of meekness—
Oh, then I am seized with a rancorous hate
And I would break down their newly-built temples

And fight for *you,* ye ancient rulers,
For you and your sweet, ambrosial right;
And before your highest altars,
Built up again, and smoking with sacrifice,
I humbly would kneel and invoke you,
Raising my arms in a prayer.—

For, even though, ye ancient deities,
When you joined in the furious combats of
    mortals,
You always fought on the side of the victor;
Now you will see that man is greater than you.
For I stand here in the combat of gods
And fight on for you, the vanquished.

. . . . .

Thus I spoke, and high above me
I saw those cloudy figures blushing,
Gazing on me as though dying;
Transfigured by sorrow—and then they vanished.
The moon was suddenly hidden
Under the clouds that rolled on darkly.
The sea came up with a rush;
And into the heavens, calm and victorious,
Walked the eternal stars.

QUESTIONS

Am Meer, am wüsten, nächtlichen Meer

By the sea, by the dreary, night-colored sea,
A young man stands;
His heart full of anguish, his head full of
    doubts,
And with pale lips he questions the billows:

" Oh solve me the riddle of Life,
The torturing, deathless riddle
Which has cracked so many heads,
Heads in hieroglyphic bonnets,
Heads in black birettas and turbans,
Heads in weighty wigs and a thousand other
Poor, perspiring heads of people—
Tell me, what is Man? And what's his meaning?
Where does he come from? Where is he going?
Who dwells up there among the golden stars?"

The billows are whispering their eternal whispers.
The wind blows on, the clouds go sailing;
The stars keep twinkling, indifferent and cold.
And a fool waits for his answer.

THE PHOENIX

Es kommt ein Vogel geflogen aus Westen

A bird comes flying out of the West.
It flies eastward
Toward its orient garden-home,
Where strange spices blossom and breathe,
And palm-trees rustle and springs are cooling.
And the glad bird sings as he flies:
" She loves him! She loves him!
She carries his picture in her small heart,
And carries it sweetly and shyly hidden,
And scarcely knows it, herself!
But in her dreams he stands before her,
She pleads and cries and kisses his hands,
And calls him by name,
And, calling, she wakes and lies half-
    frightened,

And rubs her eyes with a trembling wonder—
She loves him! She loves him!"

. . . . .

I leaned on the mast on the upper deck;
And stood and listened to the bird's song.
The white-curling billows leaped up and
    sprang
Like dusky green horses with silvery manes.
With shimmering sails, the Heligolanders,
Those daring nomads of the sea,
Went by, like lines of soaring swans.
Over me, in the eternal blue,
White clouds were floating
And the eternal sun,
The Rose of the heavens, the fire-blossoming,
Laughed at its splendor mirrored in the sea;—
And sky and sea and my own wild heart
Rang with the echo:
"She loves him! She loves him!"

SEA-SICKNESS

Die grauen Nachmittagswolken

The gray clouds of late afternoon
Sag and hang heavily over the sea
Which heaves darkly against them;
And the ship drives on between them.

Sea-sick, I keep on sitting by the mainmast,
And give myself up to a host of reflections;
Reflections that are ash-gray and very old,
That were already made by Father Lot

The North Sea

After he had been enjoying good things too freely,
And found himself in a bad way.
With this I think of other old stories:
How the cross-bearing pilgrims, in the days of their
    stormy sea-journeys,
Would be soothed by kissing the picture
Of the blessèd Virgin.
How sea-sick knights, in similar distress,
Would press the precious glove of their adored
Against their lips—and straightway would be
    cured . . .
But here I sit, and keep on chewing
An old dried herring, that salty consoler
When one's sick as a cat or down as a dog.

All this time the ship is battling
With the wild, tossing tide.
Like a rearing war-horse, she poises herself
On her trembling stern, till the rudder cracks.
Then down she plunges, headlong
Into the howling watery chasm once more.
Then again, like one reckless and weak with love,
She seems about to rest herself
On the black bosom of a giant wave,
That, with a huge roaring, comes toward her.
And suddenly, a furious sea-cataract,
Seething and foaming, rushes upon us,
And souses me with foam.

This tumbling and tossing and rocking
Is beyond bearing!
In vain my eyes strain to seek
The German coast. Alas! only water—
Nothing but water; endless, treacherous water.

As the winter-wanderer longs at evening
For a warm and comforting cup of tea,
So my heart longs for thee,
My German fatherland!
Though forever thy sweet soil is encumbered
With madness, hussars and poor verses,
And thin and tepid pamphlets!
Though forever thy donkeys
Feed upon roses, instead of on thistles!
Though forever thy high-born monkeys
Prink and preen themselves in idle splendor,
And think themselves better than all the other
Dull, heavy-footed, stupid and common cattle!
Though thy feeble old snail-council
Think they will live forever
Since they move forward so slowly;
Daily clearing their throats to argue
"Does not the cheese belong to the cheese-mites?"
Or consuming long hours discussing
"Methods of improving Egyptian sheep"
So that the shepherd may shear them like others,
Without a difference—
Though forever folly and wrong and injustice
May cover thee, oh Germany,
Still am I yearning for thee now:
For thou, at least, art good, dry, solid land.

EPILOG

Wie auf dem Felde die Weizenhalmen

Like the ears of wheat in a wheat-field growing,
So a thousand thoughts spring and tremble
In the minds of men.
But the tender fancies of love
Are like the happy colors that leap among them;
Red and blue flowers.

Red and blue flowers!
The sullen reaper destroys you as worthless;
Block-headed fools will scornfully thresh you;[1]
Even the penniless wayfarer
Who is charmed and cheered by your faces,
Shakes his poor head,
And calls you pretty weeds!
But the young girl from the village,
Twining her garland,
Honors and gathers you.
And with you she brightens her lovely tresses.
And thus adorned, she hurries to the dancing,
Where fiddles and flutes are sweetly sounding;
Or runs to the sheltering beech-tree,
Where the voice of her lover sounds even sweeter
Than fiddles and flutes.

---

[1] *Hölzerne Flegel zerdreschen euch höhnend,*

In this line Heine again makes use of a satiric and subtle play on words; *"hölzerne"* is "wooden," and *"Flegel"* can mean either a "flail" or a "clown."

NEW POEMS

NEW SPRING
(1828-1831)

NEW SPRING

1.

In dem Walde spriesst und grünt es

Now the wood blooms like a maiden
   Running to a lover's meeting;
And the sun laughs down upon it:
   "Welcome, Spring! A fervent greeting!"

Nightingale, I hear your flute-call
   As it starts the woodland ringing.
What a poignant, long-drawn cadence! . . .
   "Love"—'Tis all you know of singing!

2.

Leise zieht durch mein Gemüt

Lightly swinging bells are ringing
   With a soft insistence;
Tinkle, tiny tunes of Spring,
   Tinkle through the distance.

Fill the air and run to where
   All the flowers grow sweeter.
If you see a Rosebud there
   Tell her that I greet her!

3.

Der Schmetterling ist in die Rose verliebt

The butterfly is in love with the rose
    And flutters about her all day,
While he, in turn, is pursued by a bright
    Sunbeam that follows his way.

But wait,—with whom is the rose in love?
    For whom does she tremble and pale?
Is it the silent evening star?
    Or the singing nightingale?

I do not know whom the red rose loves;
    But I love you all, for I
Sing nightingale, sunbeam, and evening star,
    The rose and the butterfly!

4.

Es erklingen alle Bäume

All the trees are full of music;
    Nests are singing, high and small.
In this green, orchestral concert,
    Who's conductor of it all?

Can it be that old, gray plover
    Who keeps nodding to the beat?
Or that pedant who, up yonder,
    Marks his "*Cuckoo*" strong and sweet?

Or is it the stork, who gravely,
  Keeps on tapping with his bill,
Just as though he were directing,
  While the others soar and trill.

No; my own heart holds the leader;
  Well he knows the stress thereof!
And I feel the time he's beating,
  And I think his name is Love.

5.

Im Anfang war die Nachtigall

" In the beginning was the Word,
  Sung by the nightingale, '*Sweet! Sweet!*'
While grass and apple-blossoms stirred
  And violets found their dancing feet.

" He bit his breast until the blood
  Flowed freely, and from that bright stream
A tall and lovely rose-tree stood;
  And there he sings his passionate dream.

" All of us birds now live in peace;
  His blood redeemed all things that fly.
Yet if the rosy song should cease
  The wood, and all it holds, would die."

So, to his brood, the sparrow speaks,
  As though he had them all in church;
The mother-bird is proud and squeaks
  Upon her high and lawful perch.

She's a good housewife, every day
   She only lives to build and breed;
While he, to pass the time away,
   Lectures his children in the creed.

6.

Es drängt die Not, es läuten die Glocken

I must go forth, the bells are pealing;
   And oh! I've lost my head completely!
A pair of eyes, in league with Springtime,
   Have been conspiring far too sweetly.

A pair of brilliant eyes and Springtime
   Storm at my heart and have incensed me—
Even the nightingales and roses
   I think are in a plot against me!

7.

Die blauen Frühlingsaugen

The deep, blue eyes of Springtime
   Peer from the grass beneath;
They are the tender violets
   That I will twine in a wreath.

I pick them and I ponder—
   And all my hopes and aims,
All of my hidden fancies
   The nightingale proclaims!

Yes, all that I think, he echoes
　In a loud and lyric mood;
And now my deepest secret
　Is known to all the wood.

8.

Die schlanke Wasserlilie

The slender water-lily
　Stares at the heavens above,
And sees the moon who gazes
　With the luminous eyes of love.

Blushing, she bends and lowers
　Her head in a shamed retreat—
And there is the poor, pale lover,
　Languishing at her feet!

9.

Mit deinen blauen Augen

Your eyes' blue depths are lifted,
　With love and friendship stirred.
They smile; and, lost in dreaming,
　I cannot speak a word.

Your eyes and their deep heavens
　Possess me and will not depart—
A sea of blue thoughts rushing
　And pouring over my heart.

10.

Die Rose duftet—doch ob sie empfindet

The rose is fragrant—but can she be feeling
   All she breathes forth? Can the nightingale
Feel half his own rapture, half the appealing
   Poignance that wakes to his lyrical hail?

I do not know. The truth may grieve us;
   And why should we be quick to see
That such deceptions may deceive us;
   If these are lies—well, let them be.

11.

Wie die Mondes Abbild zittert

As the moon's pale image trembles
   In the sea's wild billows, even
While the moon herself in silence
   Calmly walks across the heaven;

So you wander, my belovèd
   Calm and silent; while there waken
Tears and tremblings, as your image
   Shakes because my heart is shaken.

12.

Es haben unsre Herzen

Our hearts have made a holy
   Alliance, firm and fast;
They understand each other,
   And beat as one at last!

But ah, the poor young rosebud
　　That lent your bosom grace,
Our helpless, little confederate
　　Was crushed in our embrace.

13.

Küsse, die man stiehlt im Dunkeln

Kisses that one steals in darkness,
　　And, in darkness, are returned,
Those are blessèd kisses, kindling
　　Hearts afresh where love has burned.

Sad with thoughts and premonitions
　　Then the spirit loves to view
All the past it can remember,
　　Wandering in the future, too.

But to think too much is harmful,
　　Most of all, when lovers kiss;—
Weep, my soul, instead of thinking;
　　Weeping's easier than this!

14.

Es war ein alter König

There was an aged monarch,
　　His heart and head were gray with
　　　　strife;
This poor, old monarch wedded
　　A young and lovely wife.

There was a pretty page-boy,
　　His hair was light, his heart was
　　　　clean;
He carried the long and silken
　　Train of the fair young queen.

You know the old, old story
　　So sweet, so sad to tell—
Both of them had to perish;
　　They loved each other too well.

15.

In meiner Erinnrung erblühen

In memory many pictures
　　Arise and reassemble—
What gives your voice the magic
　　That makes me burn and tremble?

Oh, do not say you love me!
　　All that may bloom most brightly,
Love and the fires of April,
　　You put to shame so lightly.

Oh, do not say you love me!
　　But kiss in quiet closes,
And laugh when, in the morning,
　　I show you withered roses.

16.

Morgens send' ich dir die Veilchen

Every day I send you violets
　　Which I found in woods at dawn;
And at evening I bring roses
　　Which I plucked when day was gone.

New Spring

Do you know what these two flowers
   Say, if you can read them right?
Through the day you shall be faithful
   And shall love me through the night.

17.

Der Brief, den du geschrieben

Your letter does not move me
   Although the words are strong;
You say you will not love me—
   But ah, the letter's long . . .

Twelve pages, neat and double!
   A little essay! Why,
One never takes such trouble
   To write a mere good-bye.

18.

Sorge nie, dass ich verrate

Do not fear that I'll betray my
   Love for you. The world ignores
What I say about your beauty
   When I gush in metaphors.

Underneath a glade of flowers
   In a hushed and hidden field,
Lies our warm and glowing secret,
   Burning bright—but still concealed.

Though the rose may flame too boldly,
   Never fear—they will not see!
For the world believes that fire
   Only burns in "poetry."

19.

Sterne mit den goldnen Füsschen

Stars with golden feet are walking
  Through the skies with footsteps light,
Lest they wake the earth below them,
  Sleeping in the lap of night.

All the silent forests listen;
  Every leaf's a small, green ear;
And the dreaming mountain stretches
  Shadowy arms that reach me here.

Hush, who called there? . . . My heart trembles
  As the dying echoes fail.
Was it my beloved, or was it
  Just a lonely nightingale?

20.

Die holden Wünsche blühen

The sweet desires blossom
  And fade, and revive and spend
Their beauty and wither, and blossom—
  And so on, to the end.

I know this, and it saddens
  My love and all its zest . . .
My heart's so wise and clever
  It bleeds away in my breast.

A MISCELLANY
(1832-1839)

SERAPHINE

1.

An dem stillen Meeresstrande

Night has come with silent footsteps,
  On the beaches by the ocean;
And the waves, with curious whispers,
  Ask the moon, "Have you a notion

"Who that man is? Is he foolish,
  Or with love is he demented?
For he seems so sad and cheerful,
  So cast down yet so contented."

And the moon, with shining laughter,
  Answers them, "If you must know it,
He is both in love *and* foolish;
  And, besides that, he's a poet!"

2.

Dass du mich liebst, das wusst' ich

  I was aware you loved me,
    I knew it long, my dear;
  Yet, when at last you said it,
    My heart was torn with fear.

I climbed high up the mountain,
　And sang a joyful air;
I walked the seashore weeping
　To see the sunset there.

My heart's the sun; it blazes
　High in the heavens above,
And sinks, immense and glowing,
　In a burning sea of love.

3.

Auf diesen Felsen bauen wir

Upon these rocks we shall erect
　A church, superb and splendid,
Built on the third New Testament . . .
　The sufferings are ended.

Ended at last the difference
　Between us, false and shoddy;
Ended the stupid rage of flesh,
　The torments of the body.

Listen how God in that dark sea
　Speaks with a thousand voices,
How, in the thousand-lighted skies,
　His loveliness rejoices.

God's beauty moves through light and dark,
　Through bright and secret places;
His spirit lives in all that is—
　Even in our embraces.

4.

Schattenküsse, Schattenliebe

Shadow-love and shadow-kisses,
   Shadow-life—you think it strange!
Fool! Did you imagine this is
   Fixed and constant; free from change?

Everything we love and cherish
   Like a dream, goes hurrying past;
While the hearts forget and perish,
   And the eyes are closed at last.

5.

Das Fräulein stand am Meere

Upon the shore, a maiden
   Sighs with a troubled frown;
She seems so sorrow-laden
   To see the sun go down.

Don't let the old thing grieve you,
   Look up and smile, my dear;
For, though in front he may leave you,
   He'll rise again in the rear.

6.

Mit schwarzen Segeln segelt mein Schiff

With great, black sails my ship sails on,
   On through a storming sea;
You know how deathly sick I am,
   And how you have tortured me.

But you are faithless as the wind
  That rushes fast and free . . .
With great, black sails my ship sails on,
  On through a storming sea.

7.

Wie schändlich du gehandelt

I've told no man how shameful
  You were, and how malicious;
But I have sailed away to the sea
  And told it to the fishes.

Upon the land I've left your
  Good name, so none may doubt you.
But through the length and depth of the
    sea,
  Everyone knows about you!

8.

Es ziehen die brausenden Wellen

The waves draw in and stumble
  Upon the strand;
They crumble as they tumble
  Over the sand.

With strength and an increasing
  Power they roar;
Their energy's unceasing—
  What is it for?

9.

Es ragt ins Meer der Runenstein

The runic stone juts into the sea;
   I sit beside it, dreaming.
The sea-gulls cry, the waves run free,
   The wind is whistling and screaming.

Many have been beloved by me,
   Many I thought were unfailing.
Where are they now? . . . The waves
      run free;
   The wind is whistling and wailing.

10.

Das Meer erstrahlt im Sonnenschein

The sea is sparkling in the sun,
   Golden and glad to be.
My brothers, when I come to die,
   Bury me in the sea.

For I have always loved it; yes,
   And it was kind to me;
It cooled my heart, how often!
   We were good friends, were we.

ANGÉLIQUE

1.

Wie rasch du auch vorüberschrittest

Although you hurried coldly past me,
   Your eyes looked backward and askance;
Your lips were curiously parted,
   Though stormy pride was in your glance.

Would I had never tried to hold you,
   Nor seek your white and flowing train!
Would I had never found your footsteps,
   Or seeking them, had sought in vain!

Now, all your pride and wildness vanished,
   You are as tame as one could be;
Gentle, and sweet beyond endurance—
   And, worse, you are in love with me!

2.

Wie entwickeln sich doch schnelle

How from such a chance beginning
   And in what a casual fashion,
There has grown so close a union,
   Such a great and tender passion.

Every day this charming creature
   Holds me faster in her power,
And the feeling that I love her
   Grows upon me hour by hour.

A Miscellany

And her soul has beauty? Frankly,
    That's a matter of opinion;
But I'm quite sure of the other
    Charms she shows to me, her minion.

Those white lips and that white forehead!
    Nose that wrinkles on occasion,
When her lips curve into laughter—
    And how swift is their persuasion!

3.

Ach, wie schön bist du, wenn traulich

Ah, how sweet you are, confiding
    All your thoughts in me, your lover,
When, with noble words and phrases,
    Your impulsive mind runs over.

When you tell me that your thoughts are
    Large and of a lofty fashion;
How your heart's pride, not too stubborn,
    Is at war with your compassion.

How you'd never give yourself for
    Millions—no, you could not bear it!
Ere you sold yourself for money
    You would rather die, you swear it! . . .

And I look at you and listen,
    And I listen till you've finished;
Like a thoughtful, silent statue
    Whose belief is undiminished.

4.

Ich halte ihr die Augen zu

I close her eyes, and keep them tight
    Whene'er we come to kiss;
Her laughter, curious and bright,
    Asks me the cause of this.

From early morn till late at night
    She questions why it is
I close her eyes and keep them tight
    Whene'er we come to kiss.

I do not even know—not quite,
    What my own reason is—
I close her eyes, and keep them tight
    Whene'er we come to kiss.

5.

Wenn ich, beseligt von schönen Küssen

When in your arms and in our kisses
    I find Love's sweet and happiest season,
My Germany you must never mention—
    I cannot bear it: there is a reason.

Oh, silence your chatter on anything German;
    You must not plague me or ask me to share it.
Be still when you think of my home or my kindred—
    There is a reason: I cannot bear it.

The oaks are green, and the German women
    Have smiling eyes that know no treason;
They speak of Love and Faith and Honor!
    I cannot bear it—there is a reason.

6.

Fürchte nichts, geliebte Seele

Do not fear, my love; no danger
    Ever will approach us here;
Fear no thief or any stranger—
    See, I lock the door, my dear.

Do not fear the wind that's quarreling,
    For these walls are strong and stout;
To prevent a fire, my darling,—
    See, I blow the candle out.

Let my arms fold close and thickly
    Here about your neck and all—
One can catch a cold so quickly
    In the absence of a shawl.

7.

Schaff mich nicht ab, wenn auch den Durst

Don't send me off, now that your thirst
    Is quenched, and all seems stale to you;
Keep me a short three months or more,
    Then I'll be sated too.

If now you will not be my love
  Then try to be my friend;
Friendship is something that may come
  When Love comes to an end.

8.

Dieser Liebe toller Fasching

This mad carnival of loving,
This wild orgy of the flesh,
Ends at last and we two, sobered,
Look at one another, yawning.

Emptied the inflaming cup
That was filled with sensuous potions,
Foaming, almost running over—
Emptied is the flaming cup.

All the violins are silent
That impelled our feet to dancing,
To the giddy dance of passion—
Silent are the violins.

All the lanterns now are darkened
That once poured their streaming brilliance
On the masquerades and mummers—
Darkened now are all the lanterns.

And to-morrow is Ash Wednesday,
And I put a cross of ashes
On your lovely brow, and tell you:
"Woman, you are dust. Remember!"

HORTENSE

1.

Wir standen an der Strasseneck

We stood upon the corner, where,
　For upwards of an hour,
We spoke with soulful tenderness
　Of love's transcending power.

Our fervors grew; a hundred times
　Impassioned oaths we made there.
We stood upon the corner—and,
　Alas, my love, we stayed there!

The goddess Opportunity,
　A maid, alert and sprightly,
Came by, observed us standing there . . .
　And passed on, laughing lightly.

2.

In meinen Tagesträumen

In all my dreams by daylight
　And nights that follow after,
My spirit throbs and rings with
　Your long and lovely laughter.

Remember Montmorency?
　The ass you dared not straddle?
And how, into the thistles,
　You fell from that high saddle?

The donkey stood there browsing
  Upon the thorns thereafter—
Always will I remember
  Your long and lovely laughter.

3.
Steht ein Baum im schönen Garten

She Speaks:
Deep within a lovely garden
  There's an apple on a tree;
And, about the boughs, a serpent
  Coils itself and looks at me.
I can't take my eyes from off it,
  While I hear its gentle hiss,
While its eyes burn with a promise
  And a prophecy of bliss.

The Other Speaks:
'Tis the fruit of life you see there,
  Taste it, do not let it fall;
Lest you throw away a lifetime
  Without knowing life at all.
Come, my darling, my sweet pigeon,
  Taste it, taste it, do not fear;
Follow my advice and thank me.
  Trust your wise old aunt, my dear.

4.
Nicht lange täuschte mich das Glück

The words you keep repeating
  How vain and false they seem;
As empty as the fleeting
  Enchantments of a dream.

For Morning comes . . . How splendid,
   After the mists, the Sun!
And lo, so soon is ended
   What scarcely had begun.

YOLANDA AND MARIE

1.

In welche soll ich mich verlieben

Which of them shall I fall in love with?
   Both of them make my senses swirl.
The mother's still a lovely woman;
   The daughter's an enchanting girl.

In those white arms and virgin beauties
   My trembling heart is almost caught!
But thrilling too are genial glances
   That understand each casual thought.

My heart resembles our gray brother,
   Who stands, a jackass self-confessed,
Between two bundles of his fodder,
   Deciding which may taste the best.

2.

Vor der Brust die trikoloren

Flowers on your breast—I heed 'em!
   For the tricolor explains:
"This proud heart exults in freedom,
   And it cannot live in chains."

Queen Marie, though I adore you,
    Listen well, though you are crowned:
Many that have reigned before you
    Have been shamefully dethroned!

3.

Jugend, die mir täglich schwindet

Youth is leaving me; but daily
    By new courage it's replaced;
And my bold arm circles gaily
    Many a young and slender waist.

Some were shocked and others pouted;
    Some grew wroth—but none denied.
Flattery has always routed
    Lovely shame and stubborn pride.

Yet the best is gone. Too late, I'd
    Give my soul for it, in truth.
Can it be the blundering, great-eyed,
    Sweet stupidity of youth?

EMMA

1.

Er steht so starr wie ein Baumstamm

He stands as stark as a tree-trunk
    In wind and frost and heat;
His arms reach up to the heavens,
    Into the ground, his feet.

A Miscellany

Thus suffers and stands Bagaritha,
  But Brahma will end his woe;
Down from the heights of heaven
  He lets the Ganges flow.

But I, beloved, must suffer
  Worse torments and in vain. . . .
Your eyes, that are my heaven,
  Shed not a drop of rain.

2.

Emma, sage mir die Wahrheit

Emma, tell me, tell me truly:
  Was it Love that made me foolish?
  Or is Love itself the simple
Consequence of all my folly?

Oh, I'm troubled, darling Emma,
  Troubled by my foolish passion,
  Troubled by my passionate folly—
Most of all, by this dilemma.

3.

Schon mit ihren schlimmsten Schatten

Now with shadows, dull and dreary,
  Evil night is creeping on;
Now our souls are worn and weary,
  Weary-eyed we sit and yawn.

You grow old and I grow older,
  And our Spring has lost its grace.
You grow cold and I grow colder
  As the Winter comes apace.

Ah, the end is sad; the tearless
  Sighs when Love begins to pall.
So, when Life grows cold and cheerless
  Let Death come and end it all.

CATHERINE

1.

Ein schöner Stern geht auf in meiner Nacht

A lovely star has risen in my night,
A star of smiling comfort and delight,
  A golden promise to the eye—
    O, do not lie!

As the young moon draws up the swelling sea,
My soul is drawn to you, and wild and free
  It bursts into a passionate cry—
    "O, do not lie!"

2.

Du liegst mir so gern im Arme

You lie in my arms so gladly,
  The cries of the world seem far.
I am your own dear Heaven,
  You are my dearest star.

Below us the foolish people
  Quibble and quarrel and fight;
They shriek and bellow and argue—
  And all of them are right.

With jingling bells on their fool's caps,
   They rise from their stupid beds;
Swinging their clubs in anger,
   They crack each other's heads.

But we, we two are lucky
   That they are all so far—
You bury within its heaven
   Your head, my dearest star!

3.

Ich liebe solche weisse Glieder

I love this white and slender body,
   These limbs that answer Love's caresses,
Passionate eyes, and forehead covered
   With heavy waves of thick, black tresses.

You are the very one I've searched for
   In many lands, in every weather.
You are my sort; you understand me;
   As equals we can talk together.

In me you've found the man you care for.
   And, for a while, you'll richly pay me
With kindness, kisses and endearments—
   And then, as usual, you'll betray me.

KITTY

1.

Augen, die ich längst vergessen

Eyes that I had long forgotten
  Snare me with their old romances;
And once more I am held captive
  By a maiden's tender glances.

Now her kisses bear me backward
  To the time we lived so sweetly,
When the days were spent in folly
  And the nights in love completely.

2.

Mir redet ein die Eitelkeit

Your love for me (so says my pride)
  Is of a godlike fashion;
But deeper wisdom tells me that
  It's only your compassion.

You give me more than is my due
  When others underrate me;
And you are doubly sweet and kind
  Because they wound and hate me.

You are so fond, you are so fair,
  Your goodness overpowers!
Your speech is music, and your words
  More perfumed than the flowers

A Miscellany

You are a friendly star to me,
   Shining with gentle gladness;
You make this earthly night less black,
   And sweeten all my sadness.

3.

Es glänzt so schön die sinkende Sonne

The sun is fair when it sinks in splendor,
   Yet fairer still are your eyes that shine—
Your beaming eyes and this splendid sunset
   Illumine and trouble this heart of mine.

For the sunset means an end and a parting;
   Night for the heart, and an endless woe.
And soon, between your eyes and my heart, love,
   The wide and darkening sea shall flow.

4.

Er ist so herzbeweglich

Her letter leaves me breathless—
   She says (at least she writes me)
   Her love, that so delights me,
Is timeless, speechless, deathless.

She's bored and dull and sickly
   And never will recover
   Unless . . . "You must come over
To England, yes—and quickly!"

5.

Es läuft dahin die Barke

Swift as a deer, my bark
  Cuts through the waters, leaping
  Over the Thames, and sweeping
Us on to Regent's Park.

There lives my darling Kitty,
  Whose love is never shoddy;
  Who has the whitest body
In West End or the City.

She smiles, expecting me there,
  And fills the water-kettle,
  And wheels the tiny settle
Forward—and we have tea there!

6.

Das Glück, das gestern mich geküsst

The joy that kissed me yesterday
  Has disappeared already;
Long years ago I found it so:
  True love is never steady.

Oft curiosity has drawn
  Some lovely ladies toward me;
But when they looked deep in my heart
  They left, and then abhorred me.

Some have grown pale before they went,
   And some with laughter cleft me;
But only Kitty really cared—
   She wept before she left me.

JENNY

Ich bin nun fünfunddreissig Jahr' alt

My years now number five and thirty
   And you are scarce fifteen, you sigh . . .
Yet Jenny, when I look upon you,
   The old dream wakes that will not die.

In eighteen-seventeen a maiden
   Became my sweetheart, fond and true;
Strangely like yours her form and features,
   She even wore her hair like you.

That year, before I left for college,
   I said, " My own, it will not be
Long till I come back home;—be faithful! "
   " You are my world," she answered me.

Three years I toiled, three years I studied,
   And then—it was the first of May—
In Göttingen the tidings reached me:
   My love had married and gone away.

It was the first of May! With laughter
   The Spring came dancing through the world.
Birds sang; and in the quickening sunshine
   Worms stretched themselves and buds uncurled.

And only I grew pale and sickly,
　　Dead to all beauties and delights;
And only God knows how I suffered
　　And tossed throughout those wretched nights.

But still I lived. And now my health is
　　Strong as an oak that seeks the sky. . . .
Yet, Jenny, when I look upon you,
　　The old dream wakes that will not die.

ABROAD

I.

O, des liebenswürd'gen Dichters

"Oh this dear, delightful poet
　　Whose great poems charm and cheer us!
How we'd love to make him happy
　　If we only had him near us!"

While these dear, delightful ladies
　　Promise me a sweet existence,
I am in a foreign country,
　　Pining safely at a distance.

What's the good to know, up North, it's
　　Fairer in the South than this is . . .
And a hungry heart can't feed on
　　Promissory, verbal kisses.

2.

Du bist ja heut so grambefangen

To-day you are so plunged in sorrow,
  I've never seen you more depressed.
Your tears have almost made a furrow;
  The sobs still shake within your breast.

Are all your cheerless thoughts still turning
  To where your home once used to stand?
Confess, how often you've been yearning
  For your belovèd Fatherland.

Do you still think of her who sweetly,
  With little scoldings, bound you fast?
And how you raged, and how completely
  You both made peace and kissed at last.

Do you still think of friends who sought you,
  And cherished you through good and ill,
When storms of inner turmoil caught you,
  Although your trembling lips were still?

And are you thinking of your mother
  And sister, dear as no one else? . . .
Ah now, I think that memories smother
  Your pride, and all your hardness melts.

And are you thinking of that fated
  Old garden where you often groped
Among the boughs and dreams—and waited
  And trembled anxiously—and hoped. . . .

The hour is late. The night is shining
    With snow that gleams like splintered glass.
And I must cease this aimless pining,
    And dress for company. Alas!

3.

Ich hatte einst ein schönes Vaterland

I had, long since, a lovely Fatherland . . .
    The oaks would gleam
And touch the skies; the violets would nod.
    It was a dream.

You'd kiss me, and in German you would say
    (Oh joy supreme—
How sweet the sound of it!) *"Ich liebe dich"* . . .
    It was a dream.

TRAGEDY

1.

Entflieh mit mir und sei mein Weib

"Oh fly with me and be my love,
Rest on my heart, and never rouse;
And in strange lands my heart shall be
Thy fatherland and father's house.

"But if you stay, then I die here,
And you shall weep and wring your hands;
And even in your father's house
You shall be living in strange lands."

A Miscellany

2.

Es fiel ein Reif in der Frühlingsnacht

(A genuine folk-song; heard by Heine on the Rhine)

The hoar-frost fell on a night in Spring,
It fell on the young and tender blossoms ...
And they have withered and perished.

A boy and a girl were once in love;
They fled from the house into the world—
They told neither father nor mother.

They wandered here and they wandered there—
They had neither luck nor a star for guide ...
And they have withered and perished.

3.

Auf ihrem Grab da steht eine Linde

Upon their grave a tree stands now
With winds and birds in every bough;
And in the green place under it
The miller's boy and his sweetheart sit.

The winds grow tender, soft and clinging,
And softly birds begin their singing.
The prattling sweethearts grow silent and sigh,
And fall to weeping—neither knows why.

BALLADS
(1839-1842)

A WOMAN

Sie hatten sich beide so herzlich lieb

They loved each other beyond belief—
She was a strumpet, he was a thief;
Whenever she thought of his tricks, thereafter
She'd throw herself on the bed with laughter.

The day was spent with a reckless zest;
At night she lay upon his breast.
So when they took him, a moment after,
She watched at the window—with laughter.

He sent word pleading, "Oh come to me,
I need you, need you bitterly,
Yes, here and in the hereafter."
Her little head shook with laughter.

At six in the morning they swung him high;
At seven the turf on his grave was dry;
At eight, however, she quaffed her
Red wine and sang with laughter!

SPRING FESTIVAL

Das ist des Frühlings traurige Lust!

It is the Springtime's wild unrest.
   Blossoming maidens everywhere
   Storm through the woods with streaming
      hair;
Echoing, as they beat their breast,
      "Adonis—Adonis!"

As dusk grows thick, the torches flare
  And frantic voices fill the night.
    With wails, mad laughter, sudden fright,
They seek him, shouting everywhere:
      "Adonis—Adonis!"

And he, that boy of beauty, lies
  Upon the ground, so strangely dead;
    His blood stains all the flowers red,
And every wind, lamenting, cries:
      "Adonis—Adonis!"

THE ADJURATION

Der junge Franziskaner sitzt

The young Franciscan sits alone
  Within his cloister-cell;
He reads a book of magic called
  "The Mastery of Hell."

And as the midnight hour strikes,
  He raves and calls upon
The powers of the Underworld,
  And cries, distraught and wan:

"For this one night, you spirits, raise
  From all the hosts that died
The fairest woman—give her life,
  And place her at my side."

He breathes the aweful, secret word,
  And, answering his commands,
In white and drooping cerements
  The perished Beauty stands.

Her face is sad. With frightened sighs
  Her poor, cold breasts are stirred.
She sits beside the startled monk.
  They stare—without a word . . .

ANNO 1829

Dass ich bequem verbluten kann

Give me a nobler, wider field,
  Where I, at least, can bleed to death!
Oh do not let me stifle here
  Among these hucksters. Give me breath!

They eat and drink with greedy haste,
  Dull and complacent as the mole;
Their generosity is large—
  As large as, say, the poor-box hole.

Cigar in mouth they stroll along,
  Their hands are fat with many a gem;
Their stomachs are both huge and strong—
  But who could ever stomach *them!*

They deal in spices, but the air
  Is filled, alas, with something else;
Even their souls pollute the streets
  And foul them with their fishy smells.

If they but had some human vice,
  Some lust too terrible to see—
But not these flabby virtues, not
  This cheap and smug morality!

Ye clouds above, take me away,
  To Africa or furthest North.
Even to Pomerania; pray,
  Carry me with you—bear me forth!

Take me away . . . They do not hear.
  The clouds are wise; they never heed.
For when they see this town they fly—
  And anxiously increase their speed.

PSYCHE

In der Hand die kleine Lampe

With a small lamp in her fingers
  And a great glow in her breast,
Psyche creeps into the chamber
  Where the Sleeper is at rest.

She grows frightened and she blushes
  As she sees his beauty bare—
While the god of love awakens,
  And his pinions beat the air . . .

Eighteen hundred years of penance!
  She, poor soul, still fasts with awe;
Almost dead, because she came where
  Love lay naked—and she saw!

THE UNKNOWN

Meiner goldgelockten Schönen

My adored and golden-haired one,
Every day I'm sure to meet her,
When beneath the chestnut branches
In the Tuileries she wanders.

Every day she comes and walks there
With two old and awful ladies—
Are they aunts? Or are they dragons?
Or dragoons in skirts and flounces?

No one even seems to know her.
I have asked friends and relations;
But I ask in vain. I question
While I almost die of longing.

Yes, I'm frightened by the grimness
Of her two mustached companions;
And I'm even more upset by
This, my heart's unusual beating.

I have never dared a whisper
Or a sigh whene'er I passed her,
I have scarcely dared a burning
Glance to tell her of my passion.

But to-day I have discovered
What her name is. It is Laura;
Like the sweet, Provençal maiden
Worshiped by the famous poet.

She is Laura! I'm as great now
As was Petrarch when he chanted
And extolled his lovely lady
In those canzonets and sonnets.

She is Laura! Yes, like Petrarch,
I can hold platonic riots
On this name, and clasp its beauty—
He himself did nothing more.

AWAY!

Der Tag ist in die Nacht verliebt

The Day is enamored of Night,
And Spring is entranced by Winter,
Life is in love with Death,
And you—are in love with me!

You love me—look, and even now
Gray shadows seem to fold you;
All of your blossoming fades
And your white soul lies bleeding.

Oh shrink from me, and only love
The butterflies light-hearted,
That sport among the golden beams . . .
Oh shrink from me—and all things bitter.

A MEETING

Wohl unter der Linde erklingt die Musik

Under the linden the music is gay,
　The couples are gossiping loudly;
And two are dancing whom nobody knows,
　They carry themselves so proudly.

Now here, now there, they glide and sway
　In wave-like measures beguiling.
They bow to each other, and, as they nod,
　She whispers, gently smiling:

" A water-pink is hanging from
　Your cap, my fair young dancer;
It only grows in the depths of the sea—
　You are no mortal man, sir.

" You are a merman, and to lure
　These village maids your wish is.
I knew you at once by your watery eyes
　And your teeth as sharp as the fishes'."

Now here, now there, they glide and sway
　In wave-like measures beguiling.
They bow to each other, and, as they nod,
　He answers, gently smiling:

" My lovely lady, tell me why
　Your hand's so cold and shiny?
And why is the border of your gown
　So damp and draggled and briny?

"I knew you at once by your watery eyes,
  And your bow so mocking and tricksy—
You are never a child of men, my dear;
  You are my cousin, the Nixie."

The fiddles are silent, the dancing is done;
  They part with a ripple of laughter.
They know each other too well and will try
  To avoid such a meeting hereafter.

THE FAITHLESS LOUISA

Die ungetreue Luise

The fair and faithless Louisa
  Returned and, lightly flitting,
She came to where the lamps burned low
  And Ulrich still was sitting.

She cozened and she kissed him;
  She smiled, and tried to soften
His grief and said, "How you have changed—
  You used to laugh so often!"

She cozened and she kissed him
  Where he lay, sad and sunken . . .
"My God, your hands are cold as ice,
  And all the flesh is shrunken!"

She cozened and she kissed him;
  Tears wet her lovely lashes . . .
"My God, your hair that was so black
  Is now as gray as ashes!"

And the poor Ulrich sat there,
  Silent and old and broken;
He kissed his faithless sweetheart,
  And not a word was spoken.

POEMS FOR THE TIMES
(1839-1846)

DOCTRINE

Schlage die Trommel und fürchte dich nicht

Beat on the drum and blow the fife
   And kiss the *vivandière,* my boy.
Fear nothing—that's the whole of life;
   Its deepest truth, its soundest joy.

Beat reveillé, and with a blast
   Arouse all men to valiant strife.
Waken the world; and then, at last,
   March on . . . That is the whole of life.

This is Philosophy; this is Truth;
   This is the burning source of joy!
I've borne this wisdom from my youth,
   For I, too, was a drummer-boy.

A WARNING

Solche Bücher lässt du drucken!

You will print such books as these?
   Then you're lost, my friend, that's certain.
   If you wish for gold and honor,
Write more humbly—bend your knees!

Aye, you must have lost your senses,
   Thus to speak before the people,
   Thus to dare to talk of preachers
And of potentates and princes!

Friend, you're doomed, so it appears:
    For the princes have long arms,
    And the preachers have long tongues,
—And the masses have long ears!

DEGENERATION

Hat die Natur sich auch verschlechtert

Has even Nature altered badly?
    And does she ape what we began?
It seems to me the beasts and flowers
    Deceive as readily as man.

The lily's purity I question;
    She yields to love and seeks to stay
The butterfly that flits above her
    And bears her chastity away.

I even doubt the modest virtue
    Of violets. They have no shame,
But fling their scent like any wanton
    And thirst in secret after fame.

I half suspect the song-bird's ardor
    Expresses more than he can mean;
He overdoes his trills and raptures—
    And does them only by routine.

The truth has disappeared, I fancy,
    And simple faith has left us, too.
Only the dogs still fawn around us,
    And even they do not seem true.

HENRY

Auf dem Schlosshof zu Canossa

In the courtyard at Canossa
Stands the German Emperor Henry,
Barefoot in his shirt of penance,
And the night is cold and rainy.

From the window two dim figures
Gaze upon him, and the moonlight
Gleams on Gregory, bald-headed,
And the white breast of Matilda.

And the pale-lipped Emperor Henry
Prays his pious paternoster;
But within his kingly heart he
Rends himself and cries in anguish:

"Far in my own German country
High and mighty hills are towering;
And within their depths, the iron
For the battle-axe is growing.

"Far in my own German country
High and mighty oaks are towering;
And in some great trunk, the handle
For the battle-axe is growing.

"Germany, my own belovèd,
You will bear the mighty hero
Who will wield the axe and swiftly
Crush the serpent that torments me!"

TO GEORGE HERWEGH

Herwegh, du eiserne Lerche

Herwegh, you lark of iron!
You rise on a swift and jubilant wing
   Toward sunlight and freedom, Liberty's lover!
   Is the long winter really over?
Is Germany really awake to the spring?

Herwegh, you lark of iron,
Because your passionate flight is long,
   You have forgotten earth's condition.
   The Spring you hail with such a vision
Has blossomed only in your song.

A TOPSY-TURVY WORLD

Das ist ja die verkehrte Welt

This is a topsy-turvy world;
   Men on their heads are walking!
The woodcocks, by the dozen, shoot
   The hunters that are stalking.

The calves are roasting all the cooks;
   And men are driven by horses;
On knowledge, light and liberty
   The catholic owl discourses.

The herring is a *sans-culotte;*
   The truth Bettina's saying;
And Sophocles upon our stage
   A Puss-in-boots is playing.

For German heroes apes have built
  A Pantheon enormous!
Massmann at last has combed his hair,
  The German prints inform us.

The German bears are atheists,
  All former faiths rejecting;
While the French parrots have become
  Good Christians, self-respecting.

The *Moniteur* of Uckermark
  To madness seems to drive one:
A dead man there has dared to write
  An epitaph on a live one.

Let us not swim against the stream;
  'Twould be no use whatever.
So let us climb the hill and cry
  "*May the King live forever!*"

GERMANY

Deutschland ist noch kleines Kind

Germany's still a little child.
  The sun's his nurse; she'll feed him
No soothing milk to make him strong,
  But the wild fires of freedom.

On such a diet one grows fast;
  The blood will boil and lurch in
The veins. You neighbors, have a care,
  Before you plague this urchin!

He is a clumsy little giant;
  He'll tear up oaks, and well he
Will use them till your backs are sore,
  And pound you to a jelly.

He is like Siegfried, fearless youth,
  Who did such deeds of wonder;
Who forged his sword, and when he smote
  The anvil flew asunder!

Yes, Siegfried, you shall slay the grim
  Dragon while thanks are given.
Huzzah! How radiantly your nurse
  Will laugh and shine through heaven.

Yours shall be all the hoard, when you
  Have slain the monster horrid.
Huzzah! How bright the king's own crown
  Will blaze upon your forehead!

ONLY WAIT!

Weil ich so ganz vorzüglich blitze

What! Think you that my flashes show me
  Only in lightnings to excel?
Believe me, friends, you do not know me—
  For I can thunder quite as well.

In sorrow you shall learn your error;
  My voice shall grow, and in amaze
Your eyes and ears shall feel the terror,
  The thundering word, the stormy blaze.

Oaks shall be rent; the Word shall shatter . . .
   Yea, on that fiery day, the crown,
Even the palace-walls shall totter,
   And domes and spires come crashing down!

THE WEAVERS

Im düstern Auge keine Thräne

From darkened eyes no tears are falling;
Gnashing our teeth, we sit here calling:
"Germany, listen, ere we disperse,
We weave your shroud with a triple curse—
    We weave, we are weaving!

"A curse to the false god that we prayed to,
And worshiped in spite of all, and obeyed, too.
We waited and hoped and suffered in vain;
He laughed at us, sneering, for all of our pain—
    We weave, we are weaving!

"A curse to the king, and a curse to his coffin,
The rich man's king whom our plight could not soften;
Who took our last penny by taxes and cheats,
And let us be shot like the dogs in the streets—
    We weave, we are weaving!

"A curse to the Fatherland, whose face is
Covered with lies and foul disgraces;
Where the bud is crushed as it leaves the seed,
And the worm grows fat on corruption and greed—
    We weave, we are weaving!

"The shuttle flies in the creaking loom;
And night and day we weave your doom—
Old Germany, listen, ere we disperse
We weave your shroud with a triple curse.
    We weave—we are weaving!"

FOUR SONGS

Es erklingt wie Liebestöne

Through my heart the most beguiling
    Bits of love-songs rise and flit.
And I think the little, smiling
    Love-God has a hand in it.

In my heart he's the director,
    Calling forth its dearest themes;
And the music, sweet as nectar,
    Fills and colors all my dreams.

Was bedeuten gelbe Rosen

Yellow roses as an offering—
    And they mean? . . . A thorny **path**;
Love that is at war with wrath,
And persists, in spite of suffering.

Wir müssen zugleich uns betrüben

We laugh and we are troubled
  Whene'er our fingers touch,
That hearts can love so greatly
  And minds can doubt so much.

Do you not feel, my darling,
  My heart beat through the gloom?
She nods her head, and murmurs,
  " It beats—God knows for whom! "

Das macht den Menschen glücklich

It makes a man feel happy,
  It drains him to the dregs,
When he has three fair sweethearts
  And just one pair of legs.

I visit the first in the morning;
  I seek the second at night;
The third does not wait, but comes to me
  At noon in a blaze of light.

Farewell, my three fair sweethearts,
  Two legs are all I've got;
I'll go and make love to Nature
  In some more quiet spot.

ROMANCERO

(LAMENTATIONS, LAZARUS AND LAST POEMS)
(1846-1855)

Wenn man an dir Verrat geübt

When all men have betrayed your trust,
  Make Faith your one desire;
When they have dragged your soul in dust,
  Take up the lyre!

In what a bright, heroic mood
  The radiant chords are ringing.
The scornful heart, the angry blood
  Leap into singing!

PROLOG

Das Glück ist eine leichte Dirne

Good-Fortune is a giddy maid,
  Fickle and restless as a fawn;
She smoothes your hair; and then the jade
  Kisses you quickly, and is gone.

But Madam Sorrow scorns all this,
  She shows no eagerness for flitting;
But with a long and fervent kiss
  Sits by your bed—and brings her knitting.

THE ASRA

Täglich ging die wunderschöne

Daily came the lone and lovely
Sultan's daughter, slowly wandering
In the evening to the fountain
Where the plashing waters whitened.

Daily stood the youthful captive
In the evening by the fountain
Where the plashing waters whitened—
Daily growing pale and paler . . .

Till one dusk the strolling Princess
Stopped and spoke a hurried sentence:
"Tell me now thy name, and tell me
Of thy country and thy kindred."

And the slave replied, "My name is
Móhamet; I come from Yemen.
And my people are the Asra,
Who, whene'er they love, must perish."

From the *PRELUDE* (to "Vitzliputzli"):

Dieses ist Amerika!

This is America!
This is the new world!
Not the present European
Wasted and withering sphere.

This is the new world,
As it was when Columbus
Drew it first from the ocean.
Radiant with its freshening bath;

Still dripping its watery pearls,
In showers and spurts of color
As the light of the sun kisses them . . .
How strong and healthy is this world!

This is no graveyard of Romance;
This is no pile of ruins,
Of fossilized wigs and symbols
Or stale and musty Tradition!

FAREWELL

Hatte wie ein Pelikan

Like a pelican I fed you
   With my blood; you ate and drank me.
Now you give me gall and wormwood—
   What a pleasant way to thank me!

It was never meant in malice,
   And your eyes were never fretful;
Nothing creased that placid forehead—
   You were just a bit forgetful.

So good-bye; and, though I weep, you
   Will not care or wonder why.
Smile farewell—and may God keep you
   Just a lovely butterfly.

MYTHOLOGY

Ja, Europa ist erlegen

Yes, Europa is forgiven
   And Danaé too. What power
   Could subdue a golden shower
Or withstand a bull from heaven?

Semele was not much wiser
  When she lost her precious honor;
For it never dawned upon her
That a cloud could compromise her.

But our scorn arises quicker
  When we read the tale of Leda—
Only such a goose would heed a
Silly swan and let it trick her!

SECURITY

Liebe sprach zum Gott der Lieder

Love said to the God of Music,
  "Times are changed. I'd be a dumb thing
If I gave myself without a
  Guarantee or pledge of something."

"Yes," Apollo answered laughing,
  "Times are changed indeed. You talk like
Some old usurer demanding
  Pledges, cynical and hawk-like.

"Well, I only have my lyre,
  But it's gold, depend upon it.
Tell me, darling, just how many
  Kisses would you lend me on it?"

AUTO-DA-FÉ

Welke Veilchen, stäub'ge Locken

Faded violets, dusty tresses,
  And a band that once was blue;
Things that I had long forgotten,
  Ribbons, crumpled billets-doux—

I have dropped them, smiling sadly,
   In the flames and watch them where
Countless joys and countless sorrows
   Sparkle in the ruins there.

Up the flue go love and lovers,
   Frail and foolish oaths—alas!
And the little Cupid chuckles
   As he sees them burn and pass.

And I sit here by the ruins,
   Dreaming in the lessening light;
While the sparks among the ashes
   Faintly glow . . . Farewell . . .
      Good Night.

MORPHINE

Gross ist die Ähnlichkeit der beiden schönen

Great is the similarity between
These two fair figures, although one appears
Much paler than the other, far more calm;
Fairer and nobler even, I might say,
Than his companion, in whose arms
I lay so warmly. How divine and soft
Were all his smiles, and what a look was his!
It must have been the poppy-wreath he wore
About his brows that touched my throbbing head
And with its magic perfume soothed all pain
And sorrow in my soul . . . But such sweet balm
Lasts but a little while; I can be cured
Completely only when the other one,
The grave and paler brother, drops his torch.
For Sleep is good, but Death is better still—
The best is never to be born at all.

SOLOMON

Verstummt sind Pauken, Posaunen und Zinken

The trumpets and drums are no longer sounded,
   Hushed is the dulcimer and flute.
  King Solomon sleeps, and the night is mute.
He sleeps—by twelve thousand angels surrounded.

They guard his dreams from clamor and cumber.
   And should he even knit his brow
  Twelve thousand arms would be lifted now,
Twelve thousand swords would flash through his slumber.

But gently now the swords are lying
  Within each scabbard. The night-winds soothe
  The dreamer's dreams and his brow is smooth;
Only his lips are restless, sighing:

"Oh Shulamite! all people cherish
  My favor and bring me tributes and sing;
  I am both Judah's and Israel's king—
But, lest you love me, I wither and perish."

Wie langsam kriechet sie dahin

How slowly Time, the frightful snail,
  Crawls to the corner that I lie in;
While I, who cannot move at all,
  Watch from the place that I must die in.

Here in my darkened cell no hope
  Enters and breaks the gloom asunder;
I know I shall not leave this room
  Except for one that's six feet under.

Perhaps I have been dead some time;
  Perhaps my bright and whirling fancies
Are only ghosts that, in my head,
  Keep up their wild, nocturnal dances.

They well might be a pack of ghosts,
  Some sort of pagan gods or devils;
And a dead poet's skull is just
  The place they'd choose to have their revels!

Those orgies, furious and sweet,
  Come suddenly, without a warning . . .
And then the poet's cold, dead hand
  Attempts to write them down next morning.

Mitteralterliche Roheit

Mediævalism's crudeness
Has been softened by the fine arts.
And our modern culture's climax
Is, I'm sure, the grand piano.

Railways also are a splendid
Influence on our way of living;
For they lighten half the sorrow
When we part from our relations.

'Tis a pity the consumption
Of my spine makes it seem doubtful
That I shall remain much longer
In a world so swift with progress.

EPILOG

Unser Grab erwärmt der Ruhm

"Glory warms us in the grave."
Nonsense! That's a silly stave!
There's a better warmth than this
Found in any cow-girl's kiss,
Though she be a thick-lipped flirt,
Though she reek of dung and dirt.
And a better warmth, I'm thinking,
Every man has found in drinking;
Lapping wine, the lucky dog,
Punch or even common grog;
Sprawling over filthy benches
With the vilest thieves and wenches
That have yet deserved a hanging;
Yes, but—living and haranguing—
Worth more envy, every one,
Than fair Thetis' noble son!

Old Pelides spoke the truth:
Richer is the poorest youth
Who's alive, than lords and ladies
And the greatest kings in Hades.
Praised in many a classic tome, or
All the heroes sung by Homer!

WHERE?

Wo wird einst des Wandermüden

Where shall I, the wander-wearied,
    Find my haven and my shrine?
Under palms will I be buried?
    Under lindens on the Rhine?

Shall I lie in desert reaches,
    Buried by a stranger's hand?
Or upon the well-loved beaches,
    Covered by the friendly sand?

Well, what matter! God has given
    Wider spaces there than here.
And the stars that swing in heaven
    Shall be lamps above my bier.

ENFANT PERDU

Verlorner Posten in dem Freiheitskriege

For more than thirty years I've been defending,
    In Freedom's struggle, many a desperate post.
I knew the fight was hopeless, never-ending;
    But still I fought, wounded and battle-tossed.

Waking through nights and days, no peaceful slumbers
    Were mine while all the others slept their fill.
(The mighty snoring of these valiant numbers
    Kept me awake when I was tired or ill.)

In those long nights I have been often frightened
  (For only fools are not afraid of fear),
But I would whistle till the terror lightened,
  And sing my mocking rhymes to give me cheer.

Yes, I have stood, my musket primed and ready,
  On guard; and when some rascal raised his head
I took good aim (my arm was always steady)
  And let him have a bellyful of lead.

And yet those knaves—I may as well admit it—
  Could shoot quite well; the rascals often chose
A splendid mark, and, what is more, they hit it!
  My wounds are gaping . . . and my blood still flows.

One post is vacant! As a bloody token
  I wear my wounds . . . another takes my part.
But, though I fall, my sword is still unbroken;
  The only thing that's broken is my heart.

HYMN

Ich bin das Schwert, ich bin die Flamme

I am the Sword, I am the Flame.

I have lit you through the darkness; and when the battle began, I fought in the first rank and led you on. . . .

Round about me lie the bodies of my friends, but we have triumphed. We have triumphed—but round about me lie the bodies of my friends. Amid the jubilant songs of victory the dirge of the funeral is heard. But we have neither time for rejoicing nor for sorrow. The trumpets are sounding again—there shall be new and holier battles. . . .

I am the Sword, I am the Flame!

ALPHABETICAL INDEX
OF
FIRST LINES IN GERMAN

	PAGE
Ach, die Augen sind es wieder	137
Ach, wenn ich nur der Schemel wär'	62
Ach, wie schön bist du, wenn traulich	223
Allnächtlich im Traume seh' ich dich	76
Als ich auf der Reise zufällig	91
Als sie mich umschlang mit zärtlichem Pressen	134
Am blassen Meeresstrande	174
Am Fenster stand die Mutter	150
Am fernen Horizonte	99
Am Kreuzweg wird begraben	80
Am leuchtenden Sommermorgen	70
Am Meer, am wüsten, nächtlichen Meer	194
An deine schneeweisse Schulter	135
An dem stillen Meeresstrande	217
Anfangs wollt' ich fast verzagen	25
Auf dem Berge steht die Hütte	158
Auf dem Schlosshof zu Canossa	259
Auf den Wällen Salamankas	139
Auf den Wolken ruht der Mond	94
Auf diesen Felsen bauen wir	218
Auf Flügeln des Gesanges	48
Auf ihrem Grab da steht eine Linde	241
Augen, die ich längst vergessen	234
Aus alten Märchen winkt es	68
Aus meinen grossen Schmerzen	63
Aus meinen Thränen spriessen	45
Auf meiner Herzliebsten Äugelein	51
Berg' und Burgen schaun herunter	25
Bist du wirklich mir so feindlich	136
Da droben auf jenem Berge	98
Dämmernd liegt der Sommerabend	141
Das Fräulein stand am Meere	219
Das Glück, das gestern mich geküsst	236
Das Glück ist eine leichte Dirne	269

Index

	PAGE
Das ist des Frühlings traurige Lust!.	245
Das ist ja die verkehrte Welt.	260
Das Herz ist mir bedrückt, und sehnlich.	113
Das ist der alte Märchenwald.	3
Das ist ein Brausen und Heulen.	76
Das ist ein Flöten und Geigen.	54
Das ist ein schlechtes Wetter.	107
Das macht den Menschen glücklich.	265
Das Meer erglänzte weit hinaus.	97
Das Meer erstrahlt im Sonnenschein.	221
Das Meer hat seine Perlen.	181
Dass du mich liebst, das wusst' ich.	217
Dass ich bequem verbluten kann.	247
Dass ich dich liebe, o Möpschen.	27
Dein Angesicht, so lieb und schön.	46
Deine weissen Liljenfinger.	109
Den König Wiswamitra.	117
Der arme Peter wankt vorbei.	35
Der bleiche, herbstliche Halbmond.	106
Der Brief, den du geschrieben.	213
Der Hans und die Grete tanzen herum.	34
Der Herbstwind rüttelt die Bäume.	77
Der junge Franziskaner sitzt.	246
Der kranke Sohn und die Mutter.	153
Der Mai ist da mit seinen goldnen Lichtern.	143
Der Mond ist aufgegangen.	94
Der Schmetterling ist in die Rose verliebt.	206
Der Traumgott bracht' mich in ein Riesenschloss.	78
Der Sturm spielt auf zum Tanze.	96
Der Tag ist in die Nacht verliebt.	250
Der Tod, das ist die kühle Nacht.	142
Der weite Boden ist überzogen.	30
Der Wind zieht seine Hosen an.	96
Deutschland ist noch kleines Kind.	261
Die alten bösen Lieder.	82
Die blauen Frühlingsaugen.	208
Die blauen Veilchen der Äugelein.	60
Die Erde war so lange geizig.	59
Die grauen Nachmittagswolken.	196
Die holden Wünsche blühen.	214
Die Jahre kommen und gehen.	105
Die Jungfrau schläft in der Kammer.	103
Die Lilje meiner Liebe.	99
Die Linde blühte, die Nachtigall sang.	57
Die Lotosblume ängstigt.	49
Die Mitternacht war kalt und stumm.	79
Die Mutter-Gottes zu Kevlaar.	151
Die Nacht ist feucht und stürmisch.	90
Die Rose, die Lilje, die Taube, die Sonne.	46
Die Rose duftet—doch ob sie empfindet.	210

Index

	PAGE
Die schlanke Wasserlilie	209
Die schöne Sonne	189
Diesen liebenswurd'gen Jüngling	128
Deiser Liebe toller Fasching	226
Dieses ist Amerika	270
Die Sonnenlichter spielten	178
Die ungetreue Luise	252
Die Wälder und Felder grünen	26
Die Welt ist dumm, die Welt ist blind	52
Die Welt ist so schön und der Himmel so blau	60
Doch die Kastraten klagten	138
Du bist ja heut so grambefangen	239
Du bist wie eine Blume	118
Du bleibest mir treu am längsten	59
Du hast Diamanten und Perlen	126
Du liebst mich nicht, du liebst mich nicht	50
Du liegst mir so gern im Arme	232
Du schönes Fischermädchen	93
Du sollst mich liebend umschliessen	50
Ein Fichtenbaum steht einsam	61
Eingehüllt in graue Wolken	95
Ein Jüngling liebt ein Mädchen	66
Ein Reiter durch das Bergthal zieht	33
Ein schöner Stern geht auf in meiner Nacht	232
Emma, sage mir die Wahrheit	231
Entflieh mit mir und sei mein Weib	240
Er ist so herzbeweglich	235
Er steht so starr wie ein Baumstamm	230
Es treibt mich hin, es treibt mich her!	21
Es blasen die blauen Husaren	135
Es drängt die Not, es läuten die Glocken	208
Es erklingen alle Bäume	206
Es erklingt wie Liebestöne	264
Es fällt ein Stern herunter	78
Es fiel ein Reif in der Frühlingsnacht	241
Es glänzt so schön die sinkende Sonne	235
Es haben unsre Herzen	210
Es kommt ein Vogel geflogen aus Westen	195
Es läuft dahin die Barke	236
Es lechtet meine Liebe	70
Es liegt der heisse Sommer	71
Es ragt ins Meer der Runenstein	221
Es schauen die Blumen alle	67
Es stehen unbeweglich	47
Es war ein alter König	211
Es war mal ein Ritter, trübselig und stumm	43
Es wütet der Sturm	181
Es ziehen die brausenden Wellen	220

Index

	PAGE
Freundschaft, Liebe, Stein der Weisen	66
Fürchte nichts, geliebte Seele	225
Gaben mir Rat und gute Lehren	127
Gross ist die Ähnlichkeit der beiden schönen	273
Habe auch in jungen Jahren	136
Habe mich mit Liebesreden	123
Hast du die Lippen mir wund geküsst	133
Hat die Natur sich auch verschlechtert	258
"Hat sie sich denn nie geäussert"	109
Hatte wie ein Pelikan	271
Heller wird es schon im Osten	167
Herangedämmert kam der Abend	180
Herwegh, du eiserne Lerche	260
Herz, mein Herz, sei nicht beklommen	118
Himmlisch war's, wenn ich bezwang	137
Hoch am Himmel stand die Sonne	184
Hör' ich das Liedchen klingen	66
Ich bin das Schwert, ich bin die Flamme	279
Ich bin die Prinzessin Ilse	168
Ich bin nun fünfunddressig Jahr' alt	237
Ich glaub' nicht an den Himmel	58
Ich grolle nicht, und wenn das Herz auch bricht	53
Ich hab' dich geliebet und liebe dich noch!	69
Ich hab' im Traum geweinet	75
Ich hab' mir lang den Kopf zerbrochen	124
Ich halte ihr die Augen zu	224
Ich hatte einst ein schönes Vaterland	240
Ich kann es nicht vergessen	63
Ich kam von meiner Herrin Haus	11
Ich lag und schlief, und schlief recht mild	17
Ich liebe solche weisse Glieder	111
Ich rief den Teufel und er kam	111
Ich stand in dunkeln Träumen	104
Ich steh' auf des Berges Spitze	74
Ich trat in jene Hallen	101
Ich unglücksel'ger Atlas! eine Welt	104
Ich wandelte unter den Bäumen	22
Ich weiss eine alte Runde	39
Ich weiss nicht, was soll es bedeuten	87
Ich will meine Seele tauchen	47
Ich will mich im grünen Wald ergehn	27
Ich wollte bei dir weilen	122
Ich wollte, meine Lieder	23
Ich wollt' meine Schmerzen ergössen	125
Ihr Lieder! Ihr meine guten Lieder!	173
Im Anfang war die Nachtigall	207
Im düstern Auge keine Thräne	263

Index

	PAGE
Im Rhein, im schönen Strome	49
Im Traum sah ich die Geliebte	115
Im Traum sah ich ein Männchen, klein und putzig	9
Im Walde wandl' ich und weine	89
Im wunderschönen Monat Mai	45
In dem abendlichen Garten	146
In dem Walde spriesst und grünt es	205
In den Küssen, welche Lüge	134
In der Hand die kleine Lampe	248
In meinen Tagesträumen	227
In mein gar zu dunkles Leben	87
"In meiner Brust, da sitzt ein Weh'"	34
In meiner Erinnrung erblühen	212
In welche soll ich mich verlieben	229
Ja, du bist elend, und iche grolle nicht	54
Ja, Europa ist erlegen	271
Jugend, die mir täglich schwindet	230
Kaum sahen wir uns, und an Augen und Stimmen	139
Kind! es wäre dein Verderben	119
König ist der Hirtenknabe	166
Küsse, die man stiehlt im Dunkeln	211
Lehn' deine Wang' an meine Wang'	47
Leise zieht durch mein Gemüt	205
Liebe sprach zum Gott der Lieder	272
Lieb Liebchen, leg's Händchen aufs Herze mein	23
Liebste, sollst mir heute sagen:	52
Mädchen mit dem roten Mündchen	120
Mag da draussen Schnee sich türmen	120
Manch Bild vergessener Zeiten	65
Man glaubt, dass ich mich gräme	108
Meeresstille! Ihre Strahlen	183
Meine Qual und meine Klagen	43
Meiner goldgelockten Schönen	249
Mein Herz, mein Herz ist traurig	88
Mein Kind, wir waren Kinder	112
Mein Knecht! steh auf und sattle schnell	37
Mein Liebchen, wir sassen beisammen	68
Mein süsses Lieb, wenn du im Grab	61
Mein Wagen rollet langsam	75
Mensch, verspotte nicht den Teufel	111
Mir redet ein die Eitelkeit	234
Mir träumt: ich bin der liebe Gott	129
Mir träumte von einem Königskind	67
Mir träumte wieder der alte Traum	73
Mit deinen blauen Augen	209
Mit deinen grossen, allwissenden Augen	28

Index

	PAGE
Mit schwarzen Segeln segelt mein Schiff	219
Mitteralterliche Roheit	275
Morgens send' ich dir die Veilchen	212
Morgens steh' ich auf und frage	21
Mutter zum Bienelein	39
Nach Frankreich zogen zwei Grenadier'	35
Nacht lag auf meinen Augen	80
Nacht liegt auf den fremden Wegen	142
Nicht lange täuschte mich das Glück	228
Nun ist es Zeit, dass ich mit Verstand	117
O, des liebenswürd'gen Dichters	238
O, die Liebe macht uns selig	29
O, du kanntest Koch und Küche	28
O, mein gnädiges Fräulein, erlaubt	127
O schwöre nicht und küsse nur	51
Philister in Sonntagsröcklein	64
"Sag, wo ist dein schönes Liebchen"	143
Saphire sind die Augen dein	122
Schaff mich nicht ab, wenn auch den Durst	225
Schattenküsse, Schattenliebe	219
Schlage die Trommel und fürchte dich nicht	257
Schöne, helle, goldne Sterne	62
Schon mit ihren schlimmsten Schatten	231
Schöne Wiege meiner Leiden	24
Schöne, wirtschaftliche Dame	141
Schwarze Röcke, seidne Strümpfe	157
Sei mir gegrüsst, du grosse	100
Seit die Liebste war entfernt	63
Selten habt ihr mich verstanden	138
Sie haben dir viel erzählet	56
Sie haben heut Abend Gesellschaft	124
Sie haben mich gequälet	71
Sie hatten sich beide so herzlich lieb	245
Sie liebten sich beide, doch keiner	110
Sie sassen und tranken am Theetisch	72
So hast du ganz und gar vergessen	55
Solche Bücher lässt du drucken!	257
Sorge nie, dass ich verrate	213
So wandl' ich wieder den alten Weg	101
Steht ein Baum im schönen Garten	228
Sterne mit den goldnen Füsschen	214
Sternlos und kalt ist die Nacht	175
Still ist die Nacht, es ruhen die Gassen	101
Still versteckt der Mond sich draussen	162

Index

	PAGE
Täglich ging die wunderschöne	269
Tannenbaum, mit grünen Fingern	160
"Teurer Freund, du bist verliebt"	121
Teurer Freund! Was soll es nützen	116
Thalatta! Thalatta!	187
Über die Berge steigt schon die Sonne	140
Und als ich euch meine Schmerzen geklagt	110
Und als ich so lange, so lange gesäumt	60
Und bist du erst mein ehlich Weib	133
Und wüssten's die Blumen, die kleinen	55
Unser Grab erwärmt der Ruhm	276
Vergiftet sind meine Lieder	73
Verlorner Posten in dem Freiheitskriege	277
Verriet mein blasses Angesicht	121
Verstummt sind Pauken, Posaunen und Zinken	274
Vollblühender Mond! In deinem Licht	191
Von schönen Lippen fortgedrängt, getrieben	131
Vor der Brust die trikoloren	229
Warum sind denn die Rosen so blass	56
Was bedeuten gelbe Rosen	264
Was treibt und tobt mein tolles Blut?	9
Was will die einsame Thräne	105
Weil ich so ganz vorzüglich blitze	262
Welke Veilchen, stäub'ge Locken	272
Wenn der Frühling kommt mit dem Sonnenschein	40
Wenn ich an deinem Hause	97
Wenn ich auf dem Lager liege	119
Wenn ich bei meiner Liebsten bin	21
Wenn ich, beseligt von schönen Küssen	224
Wenn ich in deine Augen seh'	46
Wenn junge Herzen brechen	26
Wenn man an dir Verrat geübt	269
Wenn zwei von einander scheiden	72
Werdet nur nicht ungeduldig	116
Wer zum erstenmale liebt	126
Wie auf dem Felde die Weizenhalmen	199
Wie der Mond sich leuchtend dränget	114
Wie die Mondes Abbild zittert	210
Wie die Wellenschaumgeborene	52
Wie dunkle Träume stehen	132
Wie entwickeln sich doch schnelle	222
Wie kannst du ruhig schlafen	102
Wie langsam kriechet sie dahin	274
Wie rasch du auch vorüberschrittest	222
Wie schändlich du gehandelt	220
Wir fuhren allein im dunkeln	131
Wir haben viel für einander gefühlt	58

	PAGE
Wir müssen zugleich uns betrüben	265
Wir sassen am Fischerhause	92
Wir standen an der Strasseneck	227
Wohl unter der Linde erklingt die Musik	251
Wo ich bin, mich rings umdunkelt	80
Wo wird einst des Wandermüden	277
Zu dem Wettgesange schreiten	38
Zu der Lauheit und der Flauheit	127
Zu fragmentarisch ist Welt und Leben	124
Zu Halle auf dem Markt	140